Copyright

Be sure to check out Mike's other books:

Hollywood Murders and Scandals: Tinsel Town After Dark
"In the late afternoon, her friends recalled, Monroe began to act strangely seeming to be heavily under the influence. She made statements to friend Peter Lawford that he should tell the President goodbye and tell himself goodbye."

More Hollywood Murders and Scandals: Tinsel Town After Dark
"At some point in the night Reeves and Lemmon began to argue. As Reeves headed upstairs to his bedroom, Lemmon would later tell officers that she shouted out that he would probably shoot himself."

Murders Unsolved: Cases That Have Baffled The Authorities For Years
"The body was wrapped in a plaid blanket, and placed inside a box that had once held a baby's bassinet purchased from J.C. Penney's. The boy was clean and dry, and recently groomed. However, he looked to be undernourished. Clumps of hair found on the body suggested he had been groomed after death."

Murders Unsolved Vol. 2: More Cases That Have Baffled the Authorities for Years
"McLeod first stopped at a payphone, but he didn't have any money, and so he drove to a nearby restaurant that was just opening. They didn't have a phone, but the owner gave him money to go back and use the payphone. He drove back and called the Sarasota police. Initially he was told he had to call the county Sheriff, but he responded that he didn't have any more money for more calls and then said, "They're all dead.""

America's Early Serial Killers: Five Cases of Frontier Madness
"We tend to think of those early settlers as hard working, decent people only looking for religious freedom and better opportunities for their families. However, even during those times, people existed who were depraved, evil and mentally ill. These are some of their stories."

Lost and Missing: True Stories of People Gone Missing and Never Found
"Police launched a massive search, reaching miles away from where the children were last seen in all directions. However, no evidence or any of their belongings were ever found. Even if three children could

have been swept out to sea unnoticed on a crowded beach, what happened to their towels, clothes, and other items?"

Lost and Missing Vol. 2: More True Stories of People Gone Missing and Never Found

"Interestingly, it was discovered that the same day of the three women's disappearance, a concrete foundation was being poured at a hospital nearby. It would have perhaps been an ideal place to dispose of three bodies, but there is no evidence to support any such claim. It's rumored that ground-penetrating radar discovered three anomalies in the set concrete, but it has never been dug up."

Cold Cases Solved: True Stories of Murders That Took Years or Decades to Solve

"When she had been missing for three weeks, Ridulph's tearful parents appeared on TV, pleading for their daughter's release and for her to return home unharmed. However, there would be little further development in the case for four months, until the fateful day of April 26, 1958."

Executed Unjustly: True Stories of People Executed For Crimes They Did Not Commit

"That night, the chaplain administered the last rights for a child. On the way to his execution, Arridy gave away to another prisoner his toy train. It had been given to him by the warden, and was his most prized possession. During the long days on death row, Arridy would wind the train up, and then send it chugging down the corridor. Other inmates would stretch out their hands, causing both wrecks and then rescues that made Arridy laugh aloud. They would then wind up the train themselves and send it back to its carefree owner for another trip."

Table of Contents

Introduction

What a difference a few years can make. Included in this book are several cases of murders that went cold and were later solved using DNA testing. In some cases, the first authorities knew enough to secure and save bits of skin, fabric and fluids in case they could later be tested. In other cases, evidence gathering was less rigorous than it should have been and some evidence was missed and may have delayed justice.

The implementation of the CODIS-NDIS database which contains over 11 million DNA profiles of known criminals also made a huge impact on the police's ability to identify perpetrators years after the crimes were committed.

These advances have helped to provide justice for the victims and their families who may otherwise never have found out who took their loved ones from them. To have to wait any amount of time for closure must be unbearable but to have to wait years and decades must be torture.

Thankfully, forensics has advanced so much so as to make getting away with murder much more difficult. Not that it can't be done, but today we can benefit from the details of how these crimes were solved knowing that ever advancing forensic skills and techniques will continue to help to solve crimes as they occur.

Victim: Martha Moxley
Date: October 30th, 1975
Location: Greenwich, Connecticut
Suspects: Thomas and Michael Skakel, Kenneth Littleton, William Kennedy Smith

Backstory:
In 1975, Martha Moxley was fifteen years old, and lived with her family in Greenwich, Connecticut. She was in the ninth grade at Western Junior High. Moxley was a new student at the school, having moved to Connecticut from Piedmont, California in the summer of 1974.

Her friends remember her as fun and exciting, and full of warmth. Nicknamed 'Mox', she always knew what was going on with everyone, and friends remember how she always made them feel special.

She was a loyal friend, often talking with her new friends about her best friends back in California. Her classmates remember her being friends with everyone, girls and boys.

Her older brother, John, attended the local high school and kept a close eye on Moxley as she grew up.

On The Day In Question:
October 30th was known as 'mischief night' in Moxley's hometown. Children, in particular teens, who lived in the town would get together for a night of harmless pranks, such as spraying friends with shaving cream, or decorating the town with toilet paper.

On October 30th, 1975, Moxley went out with a group of friends to enjoy themselves and get in on the action of the evening. She and her friends stopped in at Thomas (Tommy) and Michael Skakel's house.

The two brothers were having an early Halloween party. Tommy and Michael Skakel had a bit of a reputation in the neighborhood for behaving badly. Moxley's friends also report that the boys often fought over Moxley herself.

Along with the Moxley family, the Skakel brothers lived in a gated community in an affluent area of Greenwich. The boys were rumored to have grown up with a lack of discipline.

The family was also well known due to their family connections. The Skakels were Robert F. Kennedy's nephews by marriage.

While at the party that night, friends report that Moxley and Tommy began flirting with each other, and she eventually kissed him. The pair then disappeared behind a fence together around 9:30pm.

It's believed that Moxley then left for home somewhere between 9:30pm and 11:00pm. Her house was only 150 yards away, but she never made it. Tommy Skakel was immediately reported as the last person to see Moxley alive.

The next morning, Moxley's body was found lying under a tree in her back yard. Her jeans and underwear were pulled down, but there was no evidence of sexual assault.

She had been beaten with a six-iron golf club, her attacker striking her so hard that the club shattered. They then used a jagged piece to stab her in the neck.

Investigation:

Given that Tommy Skakel was with Moxley when she was last seen alive, he quickly became the prime suspect. Immediately taking action to protect his family, Skakel's father refused law enforcement access to his medical and school records.

Meanwhile, given the connection to the Kennedys, the case quickly garnered worldwide attention.

Investigators identified the golf club murder weapon as belonging to a set owned by the Skakel family. They had originally belonged to the boys' mother, Anne Skakel, who had died two years earlier.

Police also found Moxley's diary, where she had written about having to fend off Skakel's attempts to get to 'first and second base'.

Police undertook a superficial search of the Skakel's house on the day they found Moxely's body. They never obtained a warrant or returned to perform a thorough investigation of the Skakel home.

Unsurprisingly, it would not be long before the family stopped cooperating with police entirely and closed ranks.

Trying to find any lead in Moxley's death, police also investigated Kenneth Littleton. Littleton lived at the Skakel home, and worked as a tutor for the family. They also interviewed neighbors, and even homeless people living off the Interstate.

No one, including either of the Skakel brothers, was charged with Moxley's murder, and the case grew cold.

Over the years, rumors surfaced that Michael Skakel had confessed to friends that he had killed Moxley that night. Both he and Thomas' alibis had changed multiple times over the years, and it was rumored that Michael had bragged he would get away with murder because of his family connections to the Kennedys. Despite this, neither brother was ever arrested. The case lay dormant for nearly ten years

In 1983 a local newspaper, The Greenwich Time, hired Len Levitt to write a piece about Moxely's murder. Even this could not create a break in the case. Deemed 'too controversial', the article was never published.

It was another eight years again before a rumor started circulating about William Kennedy Smith. Once again, the Kennedy family name was involved in the case.

Smith was the nephew of Senator Edward Moore Kennedy, himself the nephew of John F. Kennedy. Smith was already facing a rape charge in Florida, and residents of Greenwich were sure that he also knew something about Moxley's murder. Smith's rumored involvement stirred up interest in the case again.

Mark Fuhrman, a Los Angeles police detective who had gained notoriety with his controversial testimony in the O.J. Simpson trial, took an interest in the case.

Both the Greenwich police and State Prosecutors were also continuing to look for Moxley's killer, but any leads were few and far between. They allegedly did not welcome Fuhrman's investigation, concerned that his involvement would jeopardize their case.

Fuhrman believed that the local police were making their own mistakes, such as not taking a closer look at the Skakel brothers.

For their part, investigators tried but failed to convince a prosecutor that they had probable cause to charge Tommy Skakel with Moxley's murder. Attention then shifted back to the tutor, Kenneth Littleton.

In 1992, police convinced his then ex-wife to meet him at a hotel in Boston. She wore a wire to hopefully catch a confession on tape. Littleton had had a 'big secret' during their marriage, and police hoped that it had to do with Moxley's murder. The plan was to try to get Littleton to confess to his ex-wife in the hopes of a reconciliation.

Despite talking to her for over two hours, Littleton would say nothing related to Moxley's murder, and investigators had no choice but to move on. The case would again go cold and gain little ground for another five years.

In 1998, Fuhrman published his book, and named Michael Skakel as his primary suspect in Moxley's murder. Jonathan Benedict, a prosecutor, petitioned for a grand jury investigation into Moxley's death.

In May of 1998, a three-judge panel approved the prosecutor's request for a grand jury investigation. A one-man grand jury was convened to review the evidence. Such grand juries are rare, and usually only used when all other investigative options have failed.

George N. Thim, a Bridgeport Superior Court Judge, was appointed to investigate all evidence in the case. As a Superior Court Judge, he had the ability to subpoena witnesses, a power that prosecutors do not have in Connecticut.

Prosecutors investigating Moxley's murder have said that the inability to force witnesses to speak with them hindered their investigation into the murder. Perhaps this new investigation would finally uncover the truth?

Thim took testimony from fifty-three different witnesses, mostly former residents and staff from a reform school in Maine that Michael Skakel had attended when he was seventeen.

The official statement was that he was sent there after he developed a drinking problem in the wake of the death of his mother, but some believe he was sent there to hide from authorities looking into Moxley's death.

Thim investigated the case for eighteen months before announcing his findings; there was enough evidence to charge Michael Skakel with Moxley's murder.

An arrest warrant was issued on January 9th, 2000 for an unnamed juvenile, and the same day Skakel surrendered himself to the police. He was released on bail of half a million dollars, and faced the court on March 14th.

On March 14th, 2000 Skakel was arraigned in juvenile court. Although he was now thirty-nine, he had been only fifteen years old when Moxley was murdered. Despite this, the court ruled that he would be tried as an adult.

On May 7th, 2000, Skakel's trial for murder started. One of his schoolmates, John Higgins, testified that Skakel had confessed to killing Moxley with the golf club.

Skakel had also allegedly confessed to another man, Gregory Coleman, at the same time, but the testimony was lost when Coleman died of a heroin overdose before the trial began.

The jury was allowed access to Coleman's pretrial testimony. In this, Coleman stated that Skakel had told him that he would get away with murder because he was a Kennedy.

The rest of the case against Skakel was mostly circumstantial, with the prosecution calling nearly forty other witnesses, while the defense called only fifteen people to the stand.

The defense's case was largely based on building an alibi for Skakel. He claimed to be at his cousin's house on the other side of town at the time the medical examiner estimated Moxley died.

His cousin testified that Skakel was watching a movie with her until 10:50pm, with the estimated time of death around 10pm. The forensic pathologist did admit he could be off by as much as one hour.

The prosecution disputed his alibi, showing that over the years preceding the trial, both Skakel boys had changed their alibis several times. Although Skakel did not testify at his own trial, a 1997 recording of an interview with Skakel was entered into evidence.

On the tape, Skakel said that he had been masturbating in a tree outside Moxley's bedroom window, placing himself at the crime scene. The prosecution argued that it was instead likely that Skakel masturbated near Moxley's body, after he had killed her.

Prosecutors argued that after the ability to test DNA developed in the early 1990's, Skakel invented the story to explain away any chance of his DNA now being found at the crime scene.

Their theory was that after Moxley, who both brothers liked, kissed his brother, Skakel (who had by this time been drinking) became enraged and killed her.

Forensic evidence showed that Moxley had originally been struck with the club near her own driveway, but then had staggered away while she continued to be attacked. She was dragged through grass and eventually died under the tree.

On June 7th, 2002, nearly thirty years after her death, Michael Skakel was found guilty of Moxley's murder. He was sentenced to twenty years to life in prison.

Current Status:
William Kennedy Smith was acquitted of the charge of rape. In 2004, a former employee brought a civil suit against him. He was accused of sexually assaulting her, and settled out of court. He again settled with another employee accusing him of sexual harassment in 2005. He is a doctor, and also works with victims of landmines.

Retired Greenwich detective Stephen Carroll agrees that investigators made mistakes with Moxley's case. He disagrees however that the Skakels were ever given special treatment.

He puts the problems down to the fact that it had been thirty years since the Greenwich police last dealt with a murder case. Many however disagree, believing that the wealth and family connections of the Skakel family were definitely taken into consideration when deciding how in-depth the investigations into the brothers' involvement went.

Skakel appealed his conviction in 2003, arguing that the case should have been heard in juvenile court, that the statute of limitations had expired, and also that there was prosecutorial misconduct.

His appeal was rejected on January 12th, 2006. In July 2006 Skakel's attorney filed a petition for a writ of certiorari (a judicial review), but this too was denied. He requested a new trial in October 2007, which was also denied.

He was first eligible and was denied parole in 2012. His next parole hearing is scheduled in 2017.

However, he appealed in 2013, claiming incompetence against his lead trial attorney. On October 23rd, 2013 this request was granted. Prosecutors are appealing the decision, but meanwhile Skakel was released on a bond of $1.2 million.

He is monitored with a GPS device, is not allowed to leave Connecticut, and was ordered to have no contact with Moxley's family. He continues to deny any involvement in Moxley's death.

Victim: Jeanine Nicarico
Date: February 25th, 1983
Location: Chicago, Illinois
Suspects: Alex Hernandez, Stephen Buckley, Rolando Cruz, Brian Dugan

Backstory:
Jeanine Nicarico was born on July 7th, 1972. She was in the fifth grade, and lived with her parents and two older sisters (both in their twenties) in a well-to-do suburb of Du Page County, Illinois. Her father, Thomas Nicarico, worked in Chicago as an engineer, and her mother, Patricia, was a school secretary in their local town of Naperville.

On The Day In Question:
On February 25th, 1983, ten year-old Nicarico had the flu and felt too sick to go to school. Her parents both went to work and left her at home to rest. Nicarico's mother came home at midday and gave her a sandwich and glass of milk.

At this time, Nicarico told her mother that she had let a gas company man into the house when she had been home alone that morning. Patricia scolded Nicarico, telling her to never let strangers in the house when she was home alone.

She left again, giving her daughter a hug and kiss, warning her again not to let anyone in the home. Patricia instructed her daughter to call her should anyone else arrive at the house, and she would come home.

At 1:00pm, Patricia answered the phone in her office, to find Nicarico on the other end. She had seen a TV show that she wanted to talk to her mother about. She told her daughter to just hang on for a couple more hours and then she would be home. Nicarico assured her mother she was doing fine.

Patricia's phone rang again at 3:15pm. This time, it was her neighbor Dianne. Dianne had gone over to the Nicarico's house and found it empty. Patricia Nicarico raced home, arriving just five minutes later. Nicarico was gone.

Patricia searched the entire house, but found no sign of her daughter. The only living soul in the house was the family dog, found cowering in the laundry room. Patricia later said that she knew immediately that something bad had happened to Nicarico.

Investigation:
Police started searching for Nicarico, her parents staying at home in case a ransom call came in. It was determined that someone had literally kicked down the house's door and taken Nicarico, but it had not been without a fight. The tiny girl had struggled to the point fingernail gouges were found on a wall.

Two days later, police made the heartbreaking discovery of Nicarico's body. She had been raped, sodomized and murdered her body found lying along the Illinois Prairie Path.

Police offered a $10,000 reward for information leading to a conviction of Nicarico's murder, and tips flooded in.

One of the tipsters told police that a man named Alex Hernandez knew about Nicarico's murder. Hernandez was a young Hispanic man who lived in Aurora, Illinois.

Detective John Sam, the lead on Nicarico's case, visited Hernandez to interview him on March 14th, 1983. Detective Sam had a reputation as a great police officer, and was regularly the top performer in felony arrests.

Hernandez told Sam that one night when he was drinking with friends, Ricky, a customer at the bar, began talking about killing Nicarico. Detective Sam was never able to locate 'Ricky', but he did find another man, Stephen Buckley who had also been there that night.

Sam questioned Buckley, showing him photos of the crime scene. When he saw the photo of a boot print against the Nicarico's front door, Buckley admitted that he owned a pair of boots with a similar tread design.

Buckley then allowed Sam to take the boots to be tested in the crime lab. The chief of identification concluded that Buckley's boots did not match, but he did not formally record his findings in a report. It is known that he allegedly discussed them with the Sheriff.

The state crime lab tested the boots but the results were inconclusive and so they were sent to the Kansas Bureau of Investigation. There, a criminologist reported that Buckley's boots 'probably' made the prints.

Meanwhile, Sam was becoming increasingly convinced of Buckley's involvement in Nicarico's death, along with Hernandez, whom he also believed was involved. He questioned them both relentlessly, but neither would confess any involvement in the kidnapping or murder.

Detectives tried to elicit a confession through other means. They found a friend of Hernandez, nicknamed Penguin, in the Du Page County jail, charged with burglary. Penguin was assured that his own charges would be dropped in return for his co-operation.

He was supposed to tell Hernandez that he was going to turn in his uncle as the murderer of another young victim, collect the reward and then move to Puerto Rico.

He told Hernandez that he could get the same deal if he helped police with Nicarico's case. Police were listening as Hernandez appeared to take the bait. He told Penguin that he and others had committed the crime, describing to him in detail how Nicarico had been killed. He said that he could tell police where she had been murdered.

After his confession Hernandez spent the next four days taking police from house to house. Despite confessing his involvement none of the houses that Hernandez took police to were the murder scene.

Sam began to think that Hernandez had never been a part of the crime. He still believed that Buckley had been involved.

He questioned another young man from Aurora, nineteen year-old Rolando Cruz, whose name had been mentioned by Hernandez. Cruz denied any involvement, but told Sam that Nicarico had been raped and then killed with a baseball bat, her body being kicked down the stairs of an apartment building in Aurora.

Despite the fact that Hernandez could not take police to where Nicarico had been murdered, they decided that all three men had been involved in the crime.

County prosecutors decided on the theory that Cruz, Hernandez, and Buckley had gone to the Nicarico house to commit burglary, and were surprised when they found ten year old Nicarico at home. They theorized that the three men raped and then killed her to prevent her identifying them.

Prosecutors stuck to their theory, but Sam was less convinced. He believed that it was too unlikely that three separate men who were willing to commit burglary would also be pedophiles that willingly raped a ten year old.

The odds were just 'astronomical', according to Sam. Regardless of the detective's beliefs, on March 9th, 1984, a grand jury indicted all three men to stand trial for murder, kidnapping, and aggravated criminal sexual assault.

The trial began in January 1985 and was highly emotionally charged. Both witnesses and jurors broke down in tears multiple times. Some jurors also reported feeling physically ill at the brutal description of Nicarico's assault and murder.

Despite his personal doubt that all three were guilty, Sam hoped that the indictment and trial, along with the threat of the death penalty, would lead at least one of the men to either confess or implicate others.

As time passed and this did not happen, his doubts as to the involvement of any of the three men grew. Why would one not turn state's evidence to save their life? He later told the media that he could not understand why none of them folded. They were not a crime syndicate after all, just three petty thieves.

Eventually Sam became so sure of their innocence that he resigned his position from the Sheriff's department and astonishingly offered to testify on the defendants' behalf.

Despite Sam's beliefs, there was no shortage of people willing to testify that the men, in particular Hernandez and Cruz, had admitted their involvement in Nicarico's murder. The evidence against Buckley was less involved, and consisted mostly of the matched boot print.

Penguin testified about the conversation he'd had with Hernandez that the police had set up. A cousin of Hernandez also testified that he had admitted involvement in Nicarico's murder.

Both a sheriff's department lieutenant and jailer testified that Hernandez had also told them about the crimes, though their statements of what had been said varied hugely.

In contrast, the only testimony pointing to Buckley's guilt was expert testimony from a North Carolina professor. He testified that he was able to tell which individual had left a print based on the impression a foot leaves inside a shoe. She then testified that it was indeed Buckley who had left the shoe print on the door.

The jury was unable to reach a verdict on Buckley's guilt, and the charges against him were dismissed. It would not be so for Cruz and Hernandez. After seven weeks, the jury found them both guilty. On March 15th, 1985 they were both sentenced to death.

Under state law, all death penalty cases are automatically appealed. State appellate defenders were appointed to represent both Cruz and Hernandez, as they could not afford their own representation.

Tim Gabrielsen, one of the lawyers appointed to represent Cruz, has said that he went into the appeal with no reason to believe in his client's innocence. Most people he represents, he said, were guilty of something, though sometimes not that of which they were originally convicted.

As he read the transcript of the original trial, his opinion started to change. He was surprised at how little evidence the state had against both men. He now believed that the prosecution had not proven guilty beyond a reasonable doubt, and that they were just out to convict someone for the brutal crime.

Their main point on appeal would be the refusal of the original trial judge to conduct three separate trials, one for each man. The prosecution argued that it was one crime, and so one trial. At the time, the defense attorneys had argued that the case against one defendant would unfairly influence that of the others, but they were rejected.

On review of the transcripts, Cruz and Hernandez's appeal lawyers believed that due to the combined trial, each man was in effect testifying against each other. Multiple people had each testified that each man had committed the offense with friends, but as they did not name the other defendant, their lawyers could not cross-examine that witness.

Their argument was that this deprived them of their Sixth Amendment rights. In January of 1988 the Supreme Court agreed, and ruled that Du Page County had erred when it did not conduct separate trials.

It overturned the convictions and ordered new trials. However, the Supreme Court rejected the proposition that the prosecution had failed to prove guilty beyond a reasonable doubt.

In November of 1985, the case broke wide open in the most unexpected way. There was still more than a year to go before Cruz's lawyer, Tim Gabrielsen, would argue for him in the Supreme Court. Out of the blue, he received a phone call from one of the public defenders that had represented Cruz at his original trial.

A man had been arrested in LaSalle County, Illinois for the rape and murder of another young girl. The man confessed to his own lawyer that he also killed Nicarico. Gabrielsen was immediately skeptical, thinking that such unsolicited confessions never really happened.

Seven year-old Melissa Ackerman, the LaSalle County victim, had gone missing while riding her bike with a friend. Brian Dugan confessed he grabbed Ackerman while her friend escaped. When Ackerman's body was found two weeks later, Dugan was already in jail for yet another offence, charged with the rape and murder of a twenty-seven year old woman.

Dugan's lawyer, George Mueller, realizing that prosecutors had a strong case against Dugan for Ackerman's rape and murder, offered that his client would plead guilty to a number of unsolved rapes and other crimes in return for the death penalty being taken out of the equation.

Prosecutors in Nicarico's case were also extremely skeptical at first. They saw Dugan as perhaps trying to 'up the ante' for a plea bargain. Ironically, by admitting to more murders and allowing those cases to be solved, he was doing more good than only pleading guilty to a few.

They decided to test Dugan, asking him questions about details that had never been released to the media, which only the true killer could know. An hour later, Mueller returned with Dugan's answers, asking the prosecutors how he did. With many details matching, after a long pause, they could only answer that they would get back to him.

Another six months passed, and although Dugan had already made a deal with authorities in both LaSalle and Aurora Counties, Du Page County had not made any contact regarding Nicarico's death.

Mueller believes that the hold up was because it would make Du Page County law enforcement look very bad. Because of the terms of Dugan's deal, it was effectively asking for them to release two inmates from death row without absolute certainty of their innocence.

Dugan sat down and talked about Nicarico's murder directly with a state police investigator. Again, much of his detailed description of Nicarico's death checked out. He described such things as the tape used, which had not been disclosed. He also told investigators where he bought it.

He went on to describe the manner of the rape, which had also been withheld, and told them that a tire iron had been used as the murder weapon. Although it had never been recovered, pathology reports supported a tire iron as the murder weapon.

In fact, the tire iron that was provided in 1980 Plymouth Volares was consistent with the marks on Nicarico's head. That was the model of car Dugan drove.

Work records also corroborated Dugan's statement that he had taken the day off work when Nicarico was killed. He also had prior records of assaults, abductions, and burglaries, all where he kicked in doors to gain entry, and wrapped the victims in bed sheets.

There were some parts of his story that didn't fit the facts. He said he moved his car into the house's driveway, but there had been a boat parked there and Dugan would not have been able to park alongside it.

He also go some details of the house wrong, and said that Nicarico's body had been left face up, where she was found face down. He also mentioned that her toes had nail polish, where on exhumation there was none found. Autopsy results did indicate that Nicarico had nail polish on her fingers.

Nicarico's family held a press conference in April of 1987, saying that they believed Dugan was lying. Citing more than twenty-five perceived errors in Dugan's story, they still believed Cruz and Hernandez were the ones responsible for their daughter's rape and murder.

A prosecutor from their original trial, Robert Kilander, was also skeptical. He believed that Cruz and Hernandez should stand trial again, dismissing their attempts to introduce Dugan's confession.

DNA evidence was also retested and where it had previously been non-conclusive, newer testing matched Dugan.

Despite Dugan's confession and the DNA match, both men were retried. In February 1990, Cruz was again convicted. In May 1990 it was Hernandez's turn, but his trial resulted in a hung jury. He was tried again for a third time in May 1991 and this time was convicted and sentenced to eighty years in prison, rather than death.

Despite the new convictions, the speculation over Nicarico's murder and who was guilty was not yet over. In December 1992 an appeal from Cruz saw his second conviction being upheld by the Illinois Supreme Court, but then in May 1993 they heard the case again and this time ordered a new trial, it would be Cruz's third.

In January 1995, the Illinois Appellate Court overturned Hernandez's second conviction. Cruz's third trial followed in November 1995. In it, a sheriff's lieutenant changed his testimony and Cruz was acquitted.

Shortly afterward in December, the State's Attorney dismissed charges against Hernandez. Both men were now free and Dugan remained behind in prison. More than a decade after Nicarico was killed, it was finally over.

Current Status:
Nicarico's case, and the subsequent reversal of convictions and freeing of Cruz and Hernandez, would not be without blowback. Seven different Du Page County officials, three prosecutors and four deputies, were indicted by a grand jury for conspiracy.

They were charged with a conspiracy to convict Cruz, despite knowing about exculpatory evidence—that is evidence that either proves, or is likely to prove, the innocence of a suspect. All seven were eventually acquitted of the charge.

Along with John Sam, Mary Brigid Kenney, an assistant attorney general, also resigned before Cruz was found innocent. Kenney said that she was being asked to help execute an innocent man.

Cruz, Hernandez, and Buckley all sued Du Page County for wrongful prosecution. In September 2000 they settled for $3.5 million. In 2002, Governor George Ryan granted Cruz an official pardon for the crime.

Many of the local townsfolk and also law enforcement from the time of Nicarico's death believe that Dugan had help, and do not believe in Cruz and Hernandez's claims of innocence.

In November 2005, Dugan was official indicted for Nicarico's murder. He pleaded guilty, and despite his earlier agreement, was sentenced to death. His execution was originally set for February 10th, 2010, but was commuted to life in prison after the death penalty was abolished in Illinois on March 9th, 2011.

Victim: Sherri Rasmussen
Date: February 24th, 1986
Location: Van Nuys, California
Suspects: Stephanie Lazarus and two unnamed Latino males

Backstory:
Sherri Rasmussen was born on February 7th, 1957. She was a graduate of Loma Linda University, and was on the fast track for a career in critical care nursing. Tall and considered a beautiful young woman, Rasmussen was also very smart. She had been only sixteen when she started college, and by age twenty was already the nursing director of a medical center, including teaching classes to fellow nurses. Friends remember her as being very focused and confident.

In the summer of 1984, Rasmussen met John Ruetten. John was reportedly an extremely handsome young man, and friends say they were crazy about each other. Two years older than Rasmussen, Ruetten was twenty-seven and the director of nursing at Rasmussen's workplace. Ruetten and Rasmussen married in November, 1985.

Shortly after the wedding, Ruetten started working at an engineering company, while Rasmussen stayed at her existing job. The couple moved into a condo, and life was looking good.

The only dark spot in their relationship was a rather possessive friend of Ruetten. Ruetten had been good friends with, and occasionally dated, Stephanie when they both attended UCLA. They lived in the same residence hall, and were both involved in athletics.

The pair played pranks on each other, and frequently engaged in sexual acts with each other. Despite this, Ruetten always viewed their status as more 'friends with benefits' than any true romantic relationship. When the pair graduated, they continued to meet occasionally for sex.

Lazarus would go on to become a member of the Los Angeles police force. Upon learning of Ruetten and Rasmussen's engagement, Lazarus became depressed, telling Ruetten's mother that she was in love with her son. They reportedly had sex once after Ruetten was engaged to Rasmussen, but Ruetten later reported that he did this only to give Lazarus closure.

Rasmussen was suspicious of the relationship between the pair, and eventually asked her fiancé to stop Lazarus coming over to their condo. Ruetten told her that there was nothing to his relationship with her.

On The Day In Question:
On Monday February 24th, 1986, Rasmussen was still in bed when Ruetten left for work. Usually she left first, but that day she was scheduled to give a motivational speech at work, and she wasn't looking forward to it. Rasmussen didn't see any point to the speeches and found them ineffective.

Ruetten dropped some laundry off on his way to work. He considered calling Rasmussen to check in, but then decided against it in case she was taking advantage of being able to sleep in.

By midmorning he decided to call, but received no answer, and assumed that in the end Rasmussen had decided to go and give the speech. He then called her at work. Rasmussen's secretary said she had not seen her, but this was not unusual on a Monday.

Ruetten continued throughout the day to call Rasmussen at home, and although neither she nor the answering machine ever picked up, he was not overly concerned. It was not unusual for Rasmussen to forget to turn the machine on.

At the end of his workday, he traveled home again, stopping for his laundry and to pick up a UPS package. When Ruetten arrived home, he was surprised to find the garage door up. Rasmussen's car was gone, but there was broken glass lying on the pavement.

Just a few weeks earlier, Rasmussen had had a car accident and done minor damage to her car. He wondered what she'd damaged this time. It wasn't until he found the door to the house ajar that he started to worry.

Ruetten entered the home, and made a gruesome discovery. Rasmussen was lying dead on the living room floor. She had been beaten, her face bloody and swollen. Dressed in nothing but her bathrobe, she was lying face up with the robe thrown open, one leg bent at the knee. Ruetten felt for a pulse, but found nothing. Rasmussen's body was stiff and cold. Ruetten immediately phoned 911.

Investigation:
Police quickly arrived at the home, and discovered that as well as being beaten, Rasmussen had been shot three times. Surrounding her body were signs of a struggle, including a broken vase that had apparently been smashed over Rasmussen's head.

They also found a bloody handprint next to a panic alarm, and other toppled furniture. There was a single bloody smear on a CD player that had been stacked neatly with other equipment, as if it was waiting to be carried out of the residence.

No fingerprint was found in the smear, leaving police to assume that someone wearing gloves had left it. Police also found a bite mark on Rasmussen's body. One of the detectives at the scene wondered briefly if the attacker could be a woman, theorizing that women are more likely to bite. The idea was then quickly dismissed, on the fact that most burglars and murderers are men.

Despite the fact that the scene showed no sign of forced entry, based on the broken furniture and stereo equipment stacked near the stairs, police decided that Rasmussen's death had been part of a burglary gone wrong. They would tell Ruetten later that day they believed the front door to have been unlocked.

Ruetten told police that he and Rasmussen's relationship was great, sobbing when recounting that they had just gotten married. He also said that they were not having any financial problems, and that there were no problems with any ex-partners.

Rasmussen was six feet tall and had been physically fit, and so she would not have been easy to subdue. A blood trail suggested she had been shot upstairs, and the struggle had then continued down the stairs and into the living room, where she had been beaten and then bitten when she tried to reach the panic alarm, lastly being shot again through a quilt, likely to muffle the sound.

The quilt had bullet holes through it and powder burns on the fabric. Her body had contact wounds on some of the gunshot wounds, meaning that she had been shot point blank, the gun pressing against her chest.

A housekeeper from the apartment next door had heard a struggle taking place, but thought that it was a domestic dispute and did not call police. After the attack the killer presumably stole Rasmussen's car and fled the scene.

Other expensive items, including Rasmussen's jewelry on display in plain view, had not been taken. Investigators put this down to a forced hasty exit when Rasmussen interrupted the perpetrator.

It was hours later before a criminalist arrived to collect forensic evidence. There had been a second homicide that night and he had been at the other crime scene first. He collected evidence from on and around Rasmussen's body, including looking for evidence of rape or sexual assault. The bite mark was swabbed, and a cast was also taken of the bite for possible dental comparison. By the time he was finished, the sun was rising.

Rasmussen's parents arrived from Arizona the next day. They immediately went to talk to police. Detective Lyle Mayer, who had taken the lead on the crime scene the day before, told them that police were looking at other burglaries in connection with the murder.

Rasmussen's father mentioned that his daughter had been concerned about an ex-girlfriend of her husband's. They did not know her name, only that she was also an officer with the LAPD. Mayer made a note in the record, but never investigated the lead any further.

Nearly a week later Rasmussen's stolen car was found. Investigators found several fingerprints inside, along with a drop of blood and a strand of hair. These findings however, did not lead anywhere.

Two more months would pass, and then two men committed a burglary just a few blocks from Ruetten and Rasmussen's condo. Police discovered that one of the men had been armed with a gun, and they quickly became Mayer's prime suspects.

The case gained little ground and the pair were not identified. The suspects were described only as two Latino men, between 5 feet 4 inches and 5 feet 6 inches tall. Eight months later, when nothing further had been unearthed, Rasmussen's parents offered a $10,000 reward for information regarding the suspects in relation to Rasmussen's murder.

In 1986, the murder rate in Los Angeles was triple what it has been in more recent years, with a clearance rate of 65%. Few people could predict what was just around the corner in the scientific world, and what a major impact it would have on how crimes were solved.

Just seven months after Rasmussen was killed, DNA evidence was used in the investigation of a crime for the very first time. Until then, the best that forensic science could do was test for blood type in biological evidence, a result too imprecise to break a case as thousands of people in even a small area share the same blood type.

Interestingly, the first suspect ever tested with the new technology was exonerated by the results. Police in England, where the case took place, then performed a 'DNA dragnet', collecting voluntary samples from all males of age in the area. They found the killer, and he became the first person to be convicted on the basis of DNA evidence.

In the United States, at first DNA evidence was accepted jurisdiction by jurisdiction, and many were skeptical of the new science. Over time however, both labs and courtrooms became more comfortable with the new technology, and DNA became a staple of criminal investigations. The proliferation of its use in the now infamous O. J. Simpson trial would cement the science into the legal system.

Meanwhile, despite her parents making every effort to keep the investigation into her murder moving forward, few advances had been made in investigating Rasmussen's murder. In late 1987 they held a press conference, reminding everyone that their $10,000 reward was still active and available.

In 1988, her father wrote to the Chief of Police, Daryl Gates, requesting that he personally intervene in Rasmussen's case. Again, he pushed the angle of his son-in-law's ex-girlfriend. When he received no reply, he raised it again with local detectives. He was told that he watched too much television.

Despite this, they were not discouraged. Rasmussen's mother continued to regularly call the police homicide unit to check in with the case, and in 1993 they both traveled to meet with the detective who had inherited the case from Lyle Mayer, who had since retired.

The detective told them that he had reviewed the case notes, but the prospect for any new leads was poor. Rasmussen's father then asked the detective about a new science he had heard about, DNA profiling. He was even willing to pay for the analysis to be done at a private lab. He was turned down.

The detective told the Rasmussens to move on with their lives. After the meeting, Rasmussen's mother stopped calling for updates and the case was put on ice again.

In 1993 a police officer named David Lambkin became interested in cold cases. He had always had an interest in science and technology, and was convinced early on regarding the potential of DNA evidence.

That year, he was working in homicide when the coldest case ever to be solved by the LAPD at that time was closed using re-examined fingerprint evidence. Lambkin quickly became interested in how many other cold cases could be solved using new technologies.

LAPD detectives had always been allowed to work cold cases when their active case load allowed, and using newly available fingerprint and DNA databases, Lambkin was able to quickly clear several cold homicide cases.

In 1998, another huge leap in using DNA evidence occurred. The FBI launched CODIS, the Combined DNA Index System. The database gave police the ability to compare samples to thousands of possible suspects. In 2000, a grant was available to test DNA in unsolved murders.

Lambkin, along with prosecutor Lisa Kahn, formed a task force to use the database to clear Los Angeles' backlog of unsolved murders. The newly formed cold case unit had seven detectives, and Lambkin was at the helm.

When they started, the unit had 7,745 cold cases on their books. Detectives started combing the case files, looking for murders where they would have the best chance of success, such as crimes that had a sexual element where DNA was likely to be left, or a burglary, where the perpetrators would have spent some time at the scene and was more likely to have left DNA and fingerprints behind. That first sweep resulted in 1,400 possible cases, including the murder of Rasmussen.

The new unit made its first arrest a year and half after forming, and the case resulted in a guilty plea after the suspect was confronted with the DNA evidence. Four months later, they arrested their first serial killer, using a discarded sample from a coffee cup to test the suspect's DNA.

On September 19th, 2003, the unit requested DNA analysis from the case of the murder of Sherri Rasmussen. However, given staffing shortages at the crime lab, it would be more than a year before the request was completed.

In December 2004, criminalist Jennifer Butterworth noticed the unworked request, and volunteered to test the evidence. At first, all available evidence only gave her Rasmussen's own DNA profile. Then, Butterworth noticed that a bite mark swab had been logged as evidence.

When she went to test it however, the swab was missing. It took a week before the coroner's office could find it, and when they did it was not in great condition, accidently left lying in a freezer for eighteen years.

However, the tube containing the evidence itself still seemed to be intact, and so Butterworth ran the tests. This time, as well as Rasmussen's DNA, she found another sample belonging to an unknown person.

Butterworth ran the DNA through CODIS, but no hits were returned. At that point, something curious caught her eye. Particularly in the most violent crimes, most DNA evidence analysis was XY, from a man. This time, the mystery DNA was XX.

The person who had bitten Rasmussen had indeed been a woman. Having no background on the case, the significance of the result passed Butterworth by. The result was still so unusual however, that she included the fact in her report sent back to the cold case unit.

At the same time, another advancement in DNA science impacted Rasmussen's case, this time a legal one. A ballot co-authored by prosecutor Lisa Kahn gave police the power to collect DNA samples from anyone arrested for a felony or sex crime.

Tens of thousands of new profiles then swamped Lambkin's cold case unit. With all the new work, as tantalizing as the DNA clue unearthed by Butterworth was, Rasmussen's case went back on the shelf, where it would stay again for years.

In 2007, after clearing more than forty cold murder cases, Lambkin retired. Another homicide detective, Robert Bub, succeeded him. By then the unit had ten detectives on staff, and one hundred and twenty open cases. Running out of room, the detectives boxed up all cases that were not currently being worked on, and sent them back to their original divisions.

Rasmussen's case returned to her local district. Coincidently, Bub accepted a transfer to the same unit in 2008 to run their homicide unit. The unit consisted of just him and three other detectives. Compared to the some thirty to forty cases a year in previous times, the unit now handled just five to seven murders a year. This gave the detectives time to look at cold cases. In February 2009, Rasmussen's caught their eye.

Detective Jim Nuttall began reading through the records. He was four 'murder books' (thick blue binders in which notes, photos, transcripts, and other evidence is stored) in when a piece of evidence jumped out at him. It was Butterworth's 2005 report. He noted that the presence of female DNA at the crime scene completely changed the original assumption of two male burglars.

Reading through the crime reports, he noted that there were several obvious targets for a burglar that had been completely ignored, including Rasmussen's jewelry box sitting in plain sight, along with expensive stereo equipment.

Reanalyzing the scene, Nuttall and Bub, along with two other detectives decided that burglary had likely never been the motive. The front door being unlocked and the alarm off didn't just mean that there were no signs of forced entry. It also meant that someone would have been able to enter the condo without being heard by Rasmussen.

Nuttall believed that she had first been surprised upstairs, and that the shattered glass came from someone shooting through glass doors, missing Rasmussen. The glass was bowed outwards slightly, a sign that a bullet had passed through in that direction.

The most likely explanation for the bite mark was that Rasmussen had momentarily been able to wrap her arm around her assailant's neck, only to be bitten to make her let go. The vase was then used to subdue her, before she was shot. By then, it would only be minutes before Rasmussen bled out.

Originally, the stereo equipment stacked on the floor had lead Mayer to conclude the motive was burglary. But when analyzed, the smudge of blood found on the equipment was Rasmussen's. If the perpetrator had killed Rasmussen and then fled, panicked, why had they stopped to first stack the equipment? More likely, someone was trying to artificially set the scene. The case would have to go back to square one.

The detectives went back to the beginning of the whole investigation, this time making note of any female suspects. When they were done, they had five names, including Stephanie Lazarus. There was a note next to her name, just "P.O."

The detectives placed no importance on it, until they called Ruetten to follow up, and he told them that Lazarus was a Los

Angeles police officer. The admission stunned Nuttall. Did an LAPD Officer get away with murder?

Finding the record of Rasmussen's father's insistence that police investigate Ruetten's ex-girlfriend, Lazarus rose to the top of the suspect list. It was then that the detectives in the unit locked the case down. They would not record Lazarus' actual name anywhere it could be seen, and would not speak it out loud.

They were concerned both with tarnishing an innocent cop's reputation if she was innocent, and tipping off a dirty one if Lazarus had killed Rasmussen. They also promised each other they would follow the case as the evidence revealed, even if it found an LAPD officer had committed murder.

Three of the other women on the list were quickly excluded, as they had little motive to harm Rasmussen. Detectives were then left with Lazarus and one other, a fellow nurse who had argued with Rasmussen at work. Given that all the evidence suggested Ruetten and Lazarus' relationship was long over, they investigated the nurse first.

They found her living in northern California, and local law enforcement managed to surreptitiously collect a DNA sample. Two months later that report came back – negative. Detectives were now down to just one suspect, Stephanie Lazarus.

The detectives then began investigating every part of Lazarus' interactions with Rasmussen and Ruetten. They learned that Lazarus and Ruetten had both graduated from college in the early 1980's, and had dated each other for a time after that.

In 1985, Ruetten started a serious relationship with Rasmussen, and any relationship or casual sex he'd had with Lazarus was over. Ruetten proposed in the summer of 1985, and by November he and Rasmussen were married. Three months later Rasmussen was dead.

When Ruetten and Rasmussen got married, Lazarus was twenty-six years old, and had already been a police officer for three years. After Rasmussen's death, she was promoted to detective in 1993. In 1996 Lazarus married a fellow officer. The pair adopted a baby girl.

In 2006 Lazarus was reassigned to the Art Theft Detail, a highly regarded position. Lazarus' own record was clean, with not a single use of force or misconduct incident recorded on her professional record. Her husband was a detective in the Commercial Crimes division.

Lazarus was active in the Los Angeles Women Police Officers Association, and even organized childcare for families of other officers. Was it really possible that such an upstanding member of the LAPD, and a woman no less, could be capable of brutal murder?

Despite the unlikely scenario that a violent murder had been committed by a female police officer, the early evidence surrounding Lazarus was too suspicious, and so the unit continued to dig into her past.

One member, Marc Martinez, remembered that during the 1980's, many Los Angeles police used a .38 as their backup or off-duty weapon. This matched the caliber of the murder weapon from Rasmussen's case.

A police officer would be crazy to use their duty weapon to murder someone, they surmised, as you'd have to get rid of it and there was hell to pay if you lost your duty weapon.

If you were going to do it, you'd use your backup. The detectives searched the state gun registry database for a .38 registered in Lazarus' name. They found a record of a .38 in her name had been reported stolen just thirteen days after Rasmussen's murder.

Lazarus had reported the theft to the Santa Monica police department, telling them that her car had been broken into near the Santa Monica pier. The detectives assumed that Lazarus had therefore thrown the gun into the Pacific Ocean, eliminating all hope for a ballistics match.

Meanwhile, Nuttall spoke to Rasmussen's father again, who still firmly believed that his son-in-law's ex-girlfriend was involved. He told the detective that Rasmussen had said the woman even visited her at work and confronted her. Nuttall was careful not to tip his hand to Rasmussen's father, but the time had come to take their suspicions further.

The detectives knew that if the case were to proceed against Lazarus, it would end up with the Robbery-Homicide division. The division was an elite unit that took on the most high profile and sensitive cases.

Robert Bub had worked in the division, and wanted to hand them a completely professional case. It was time to test Lazarus' DNA. The detectives had discussed this before, and had considered getting a surreptitious sample, where the suspect does not know the sample is being collected.

Such evidence in the past has included discarded cigarette butts, licked envelope flaps, coffee cups, and chewing gum. This time however, they felt that the potential for a screw-up was too high, and if they were going to give the case to the Robbery-Homicide division, they wanted it airtight.

Bub then went to his lieutenant and briefed him, making his lieutenant the first person outside their group to be told a police officer was even under suspicion of Rasmussen's murder.

The lieutenant quickly brought in the captain of the local division and the chief of the Valley Bureau, their commanding officer. The decision was made to leave the case with Bub and his unit until a DNA match was confirmed.

Everything now hinged on the DNA being a match. If it did, the case would proceed up the ladder and be further investigated. If it didn't, it was likely that Rasmussen's case would be shelved again. Potentially to never be solved.

On May 19th, 2009, the detectives met with the Professional Standards Bureau, a surveillance unit who were directly under the Chief of Police's command. On May 27th plainclothes detectives were trailing Lazarus. When she threw out a cup with a straw she had been drinking from, detectives quickly retrieved it from the trash.

The recovered evidence was rushed for processing. Just two days later on May 29th, Bub received his answer. The technician at the crime lab rang his cell on his day off and told him the news – it was a match.

The detectives moved quickly. Lazarus herself worked just across the hall. The art theft bureau was part of the Robbery-Homicide division, and she knew many of the detectives in that unit. Assigning the case to anyone there would be difficult.

In the end the case was assigned to Greg Stearns and Dan Jaramillo, two detectives who did not know Lazarus well and had no perceived bias either for or against her. It was again stressed that the investigation had to remain top secret;

detectives by their nature were naturally inquisitive and rumors could spread quickly.

Within hours of the DNA results being released, Stearns and Jaramillo were being briefed on the entire case, all the way from the beginning over two decades before. Once they had absorbed the information, they along with Bub and Nuttall went to the prosecutors assigned to the case.
To help preserve the case's secrecy, Stearns and Jaramillo then began working out of a conference room at the District Attorney's office.

Nuttall flew with another Robbery-Homicide detective, Lisa Sanchez, to visit the Rasmussen family in Arizona. They wanted to get their official statement on record, as well as update them on the investigation before anything leaked from the LAPD or the District Attorney's office.

The detectives became concerned about how exactly they were going to approach Lazarus. It was out-of-the-question to take her in for questioning in the usual way, nor could they enter her house with a warrant in the middle of the night.

All were worried about what could happen if Lazarus was confronted when she was armed, which was often for members of the police force. Eventually they decided to ask Lazarus to accompany them to interview a suspect in the jail division, located one floor down from her division.

Guns were not allowed in the jail, and so it would not seem unusual for Lazarus to surrender her weapon, along with the other detectives. Once Lazarus entered the interview room, the detectives would reveal that it was her they would be interviewing.

Given Lazarus' own experience, they were wondering if she would talk to them at all, no doubt well aware of her right to silence and to legal counsel. The detective's goal was to encourage her to continue to talk for as long as possible, while also making it clear that she was free to leave at any time.

What Lazarus did not know was that this would be only a technicality. Regardless of what she said or didn't say in the interview, the detectives were planning to arrest her the moment she tried to leave.

At 6:40am on Friday June 5th, 2009, Jaramillo, who was wearing a wire, asked Lazarus to come and talk to their 'suspect'. The moment she entered the door of the interrogation room, where Stearns was waiting, she was told that her name had come up in a case involving Ruetten.

At this stage Rasmussen was not mentioned by name. Lazarus was told only that they were speaking to her in private as she was married to someone else and Ruetten was an ex.

As the interview started, Lazarus appeared confused at first as to why they would be asking her about Ruetten and his wife, stating that she didn't really know his wife, and was unsure if they had even met.

She told the pair that she and Ruetten had dated while in college. She claimed to not remember Rasmussen's name, and only knew that she had been killed through seeing a poster at work. Lazarus then listed all the men she had dated before she met her husband, making sure to emphasis that Ruetten was just one of many, and nothing special, saying that they were together a million years ago.

As the detectives slowly revealed that they knew more about her than they originally let on, Lazarus' story also started to shift. Now, she did remember meeting Rasmussen, and knowing where she worked.

She now thought they had met, likely several times. She recalled that she had visited Rasmussen to ask her to tell Ruetten to stop calling her. However, she continued to deny that she'd ever had a problem with Rasmussen, let alone that they'd ever argued over Ruetten. When told others had reported she had confronted Rasmussen at her place of work, Lazarus denied remembering ever doing that, but that it was possible.

More than an hour later, the meandering discussion lead to the murder of Rasmussen, and Lazarus was asked to submit a DNA sample. Appearing shocked, Lazarus stood and walked out, but she only made it as far as the hallway before she was placed in cuffs and put under arrest. As soon as she was arrested, the call was put in to officers waiting at Lazarus' home. Her home and car were then searched.

Lazarus was transferred directly to Lynwood Jail. By June 8th she had been officially charged with Rasmussen's murder. Many colleagues who heard the news were shocked, saying how supportive and outgoing Lazarus was. A few commented that her behavior changed when she was angry.

Lazarus was given early retirement from the LAPD, and was held in jail for nearly six months before a hearing set bail at $10 million, an amount twice that of what prosecutors had proposed. The judge cited the strong case against her, her likelihood of fleeing, and her ability to obtain weapons through her police officer husband.

By October, pretrial arguments had begun. Lazarus' lawyer, Mark Overland, moved to have the entire case dismissed, based on the grounds that the detectives should have told

Lazarus she was a suspect. He also cited missing evidence from the original file, such as interview recordings, forensic information, and also a lie detector test Ruetten allegedly failed.

Overland said that Lazarus' due process had been affected due to the age and subsequent degradation of the evidence. He argued that the truth-in-evidence provision of the California Constitution required that the long delay in bringing charges, which had adversely affected his ability to present other evidence or argue against the prosecution, be considered sufficiently negligent so as to justify dismissing the case entirely.

The prosecution however argued that Judge Perry was only required to apply federal standards, which said that such a delay could only be prejudicial if it was also intentional. The judge agreed and the case against Lazarus went to trial.

Overland's next move was to quash the search warrants that had been executed on Lazarus' home and car, along with a search of her workspace. He argued that the evidence did not sufficiently establish that further evidence was likely to be found in those places. In fact, Lazarus had not moved into her current residence until eight years after Rasmussen's death.

He argued that it was deceptive for the submitting detectives to claim they were looking for the murder weapon, when case notes showed that Nuttall already theorized that the gun had been tossed in the ocean.

While the judge did say that he was uncomfortable allowing the admission of some of the evidence, particularly items that Lazarus had accumulated after Rasmussen's death, an experienced judge had issued the warrants and so a good faith exception applied and everything collected could be admitted into evidence. Overland then requested a hearing to cross-examine the detective who requested the search warrant, but this request was also denied.

It was late 2010 before Overland's next attempt to free Lazarus was made. He sought to bar the admission of statements made by Lazarus while being interviewed in the jail division. He argued that California law required police officers to answer questions or face disciplinary action.

This entitled Lazarus to automatic immunity for any answers she gave during that interview. The prosecution argued that only applied during an active administrative proceeding, and that there was not one against Lazarus until she was arrested after the interview. Again the judge agreed.

Another year would pass, and Overland submitted his last significant pretrial motion, arguing that the procedure used to match Lazarus' DNA was sufficiently different enough from previous methods that she was entitled to a hearing to prove the scientific validity of the results. Again, his motion was denied, with the judge ruling that it was another form of the same commonly used method.

In early 2012, three years after Lazarus was arrested, the trial of Rasmussen's murder case began. Because of the age of the case, Lazarus' occupation, and the love triangle story behind the murder, the case attracted huge media attention. Ruetten's testimony was particularly gripping, becoming so emotional at times that he wept on the stand.

Overland's main defense was to stress that the original assumption of burglary had botched the investigation and left crucial evidence un-analyzed or investigated, such as a bloody fingerprint on one of the walls.

He also questioned the assumption that the murder weapon had been Lazarus' gun, when hers was missing and therefore untested and .38s were in wide use at the time.

Lastly he vigorously attacked the DNA evidence, claiming that improper storage and a hole in the tube could have allowed Lazarus's DNA to be added to the sample at another date long after the collection.

The defense also refuted Lazarus' alleged infatuation with Ruetten and jealously of Rasmussen by reading excerpts from a journal, where Lazarus wrote of her dates with several other men.

Her lawyer also presented character witnesses that denied she was depressed over the end of her relationship with Ruetten, nor had she ever shown any violent tendencies. The defense's last witness called was a fingerprint expert, who testified that the prints found at the crime scene did not match Lazarus.

As his last ditch effort, Overland also moved for a mistrial after a prosecutor told the jury that no alibi had been provided by Lazarus for the time of the murder. Under law, the defendant's refusal to testify cannot be used against them. Once again the judge denied the move for a mistrial.

After several days of deliberation, a jury of eight women and four men found Lazarus guilty of first-degree murder. She was later sentenced in March to twenty-seven years to life in prison.

Current Status:
Lazarus is currently incarcerated at the Central California Women's Facility. She will be eligible for parole in 2039, at which time she will be nearly eighty years old.

As a result of the trial, it was discovered that not all the evidence in possession by the LAPD had been found. Two lawsuits based on these allegations have been filed. One was by Rasmussen's parents, and was dismissed on the basis of being time-barred.

The other was a whistleblower suit by Jennifer Butterworth (now Jennifer Francis), the criminalist who tested Lazarus' DNA. She alleges that misconduct in Rasmussen's and other high-profile cases led to retaliation and harassment from superiors when she and others tried to report both the results found and the alleged misconduct. Francis' lawsuit is still pending.

Rasmussen's father would later say that he never liked Ruetten as a match for his daughter. Before her death Rasmussen had allegedly confided in him about Lazarus. Rasmussen believed Lazarus was trying to provoke her, and intrude on her and Ruetten's relationship.

Rasmussen told her father that she and Ruetten had argued over the matter, and Ruetten had told her there was nothing between him and Lazarus. Rasmussen did not want her husband to have further contact with Lazarus, but Ruetten would not agree.

He told Rasmussen that it was better to placate Lazarus, and refused to cut any contact with Lazarus. The last time her father spoke with Rasmussen, she told him she was going to take care of the ex-girlfriend problem herself.

Rasmussen's father says he told the police the day after Rasmussen's murder to look into the lady cop ex-girlfriend, but the suggestion was immediately dismissed.

In May 2013, Lazarus' new attorney, Donald Tickle, filed an extensive appeal against her conviction. He argued that multiple precedents supported the defense arguments made in the pretrial motions, and that the judge had erred in the denial of all four of them. The appeal was denied and her conviction upheld in July 2015.

Victims: Charlie Keever and Jonathan Sellers
Date: March 27th, 1993
Location: San Diego, California
Suspects: Unnamed child pornographer, unnamed homeless man, Scott Thomas Erskine

Backstory:
Charles Keever and Jonathan Sellers (nicknamed Charlie and Jon) were friends. Keever, born in 1979, was thirteen and had an older sister and brother.

Sellers was younger, and at nine years old was the fourth of six children born to his parents. Sellers was a twin, born just two minutes after his sister. He also had two other sisters, a brother, and a half brother.

On The Day In Question:
On Saturday March 27th, 1993, Keever and Sellers left their homes together to go for a bike ride. Seller's older brother Alton, also thirteen, was supposed to go riding with Keever, but at the last minute plans changed and he stayed behind.

Sellers' twin sister Jennifer also offered to go with the boys, but Sellers reportedly said he didn't want a girl coming along, and so Seller's mother allowed the boys to go riding on their own, telling Jennifer she could go the next time.

Keever and Sellers were both riding royal blue bicycles. It is known that they stopped at Rally's, a local fast food restaurant in Palm City, San Diego, around midday. They then went into a nearby pet store and played with the animals in the store, chatting with both the manager and other customers in the store. They would be the last to ever see either boy alive.

Two days passed before any trace of either boy was be found. On March 29th, another bike rider found Keever and Sellers' bodies. The boys' bodies were in an igloo like fort, along the banks of the Otay River in Palm City. Their bikes were also found just ten yards away, left in overgrown brush alongside the west bank of the river.

Both boys had been assaulted. Keever was lying on the ground, his head resting on both his and Seller's clothing. His genitals were covered in bite marks and blood, and an autopsy would later reveal that the injuries occurred before Keever died.

Sellers was hanging from a rope in a nearby tree. He too had suffered sexual abuse, found naked from the waist down and with damage to his genitals. His legs and arms had been bound with rope, he had been gagged, and a rope was wrapped tightly around his neck.

Investigation:
There were no witnesses to either the boy's abduction or murders. DNA samples were taken and sperm was found, but with limits on what could be tested with the science of the time, the discovery did not result in a suspect. Other evidence was collected at the scene, including two cigarette butts.

Inside the igloo-like structure, police also found a cleaned cat skull prominently on display. It's known that sociopaths often also murder or torture animals. Was Keever and Sellers' killer a psychopath? Investigators also consulted experts in Satanism, but this never led anywhere.

Without any witnesses, detectives started their investigations with a list of six thousand registered sex offenders living in the county. From there, they used any connections to South Bay and similar crimes previously committed to reduce the list down to three hundred names. Police then collected and stored DNA samples from hundreds of suspects.

A print from just the tip of a finger was found on Sellers' gag. Investigators collected prints from hundreds of people searching for a match.

Investigators also interviewed many homeless men who lived near the river. Shortly after the boys were killed, activists wanted to clean up the riverbanks by requiring hundreds of homeless people who lived there to move on.

Police knew that one of them may be able to shed some light on the case, and asked the authorities to leave the men where they were, worried that if the transient population was moved on a potential witness would be lost.

Despite these multiple and lengthy interviews and evidence collections, at the end police were no closer to identifying the killer.

To try and generate more tips and interest in the case, police purposely kept the case front and center in the news. As time went on and years passed, police received many tips identifying the guilty party.

They investigated every lead, even testing each stamp and envelope for DNA, just in case it was the killer himself who had sent it. Despite their efforts, the case remained unsolved.

In the mid 1990's, the lead investigator in the case, San Diego Police Sergeant Bill Holmes, had a lead he hoped would finally identify the killer. He discovered that there was a man who was involved in a child pornography ring found operating in Southern California.

The man had moved to Acapulco, and a federal warrant had been issued for his arrest. The man had then be shot and died as a result of the wound while still in Mexico. His badly decomposed body had been buried in a pauper's grave.

Holmes made the trip and worked with Mexican officials to exhume the body and remove a section of rib for DNA testing. It was not a match.

In March of 1994, probation officer Anne Royer had just completed a report on Scott Thomas Erskine. He had been found guilty of the rape of a woman from San Diego in the summer of 1993, five months after Keever's and Sellers' deaths. She noted that Erskine's criminal record also included both rapes and assaults on girls and boys, as well as adult women. She called Holmes and asked if police had ever looked at Erskine in the case of the boys' murders.

Holmes assigned detective David Ayers to follow up on the tip. Ayers met with Royer and received all of the information about Erskine's past. The detective later testified that he was not asked to follow up further, and so the reports were stored along with information on other potential suspects.

There they would remain until Ayers retired several years later, when they were passed on to another detective. When that detective also retired, the documents were returned to Holmes' possession.

Holmes recalled that at the time they had far more likely and more serious offenders on their potential suspects list than Erskine. The detectives had hundreds of suspects to investigate, and Erskine's records were relatively minor, with his attacks mostly being on females. What the detectives did not know was that Erskine's past was far more brutal he just hadn't at that stage been caught for many of his crimes.

In 2001, the case broke wide open. DNA evidence had been collected from Keever's mouth at the time of his murder, but at that time the technology to test it properly had not existed.

In 2001, advanced DNA technology tests revealed to scientists that someone else had left his DNA inside Keever's mouth. The DNA was run as 'cold DNA' against the database of convicted criminals, and it got a hit. The DNA matched a man who was already in prison for rape. His name was Scott Erskine.

As well as the DNA match from Keever's body, Erskine's DNA was also found on the two cigarette butts collected at the murder scene. He was charged with two counts of first degree murder, using the special circumstances allegations that the boys were killed during the commission of a lewd and lascivious act on a child under fourteen.

Erskine's trial began in 2003, more than a decade after the deaths of Keever and Sellers. As well as the murder charges, he was also charged with the special allegations of sodomy, oral copulation, child molestation, and torture, along with three counts of special circumstances of torture, sexual assault, and multiple murders.

The case was a brutal one, with even a veteran court reporter saying that it was 'one of the sickest crimes' he'd ever seen. A television reporter also fled the courtroom during the trial, overwhelmed by emotion after seeing photos of the boys' bodies.

Deliberations lasted only two and a half hours, the jury finding Erskine guilty. During the penalty phase of the trial, a sole juror did not want to find for the death penalty, instead voting for life in prison without the possibility of parole.

The judge declared a mistrial on the penalty phase of the trial only, and a new jury was convened just to decide Erskine's sentence in April 2004. This time, the vote for the death penalty was unanimous and on September 1st, 2004 the judge sentenced Erskine to death.

Current Status:
Before Erskine was arrested for the murder, Keever's mother, Maria, held her own investigation into the boys' murders. She went as far as to obtain a gun, go undercover as a homeless person, and then eventually lead police to her own suspect. The police exonerated her suspect.

Milena Sellers, Jonathan Sellers' mother, was thankful after the verdict. Sadly, Keever's father died before his son's murderer was brought to justice.

Keever and Sellers' murder would not be the only cold case solved by bringing Erskine to justice. While he was awaiting trial for the boys' murder, investigators in Florida ran DNA found on a cigarette at the scene of the murder of twenty-six year old Renee Baker.

Foreign DNA was also found on swabs taken from the inside of her mouth. Baker had been killed on June 23rd, 1989, but no one had ever been arrested for her murder. The DNA matched Erskine's. In 2003, he was formally charged with her murder.

In 2004 he made a plea deal with authorities, agreeing to be interviewed about the unsolved murder of another woman in 1989. In return, he was sentenced to life in prison for the murder of Baker. Just one month later, he was sentenced to death for the murder of Keever and Sellers.

Victims: Members of the 16th Street Baptist Church
Date: September 15th, 1965
Location: Birmingham, Alabama
Suspects: The Cahaba Boys (KKK splinter group), including Thomas Blanton Jr., Robert Chambliss, Herman Frank Cash, and Bobby Cherry. Gary Thomas Rowe, Jr.

Backstory:
The bombing of the 16th Street Baptist Church in Alabama in 1965 was a pivotal moment in the Civil Rights Movement. It triggered violence to break out in the streets, and in the end contributed much support to the passing of the Civil Rights Act in 1964.

Birmingham, Alabama was a major player in the Civil Rights Movement in the 1960's. Many protests, marches, and sit-ins were held there. These events were often met with violence and brutality both from white town citizens and the police themselves.

On June 11th that same year, President John F. Kennedy took control of the Alabama National Guard to prevent Governor George Wallace from blocking the desegregation of schools in Birmingham. Wallace forbade two black students from entering the building while trying to register at the University of Alabama.

Birmingham was founded in 1871 and grew rapidly to become an important industrial and commercial center for Alabama. However, it was also one of the most racially segregated and discriminatory cities in America well into the late 1960's.

The city was home to one of the most violent chapters of the Ku Klux Klan (KKK), and the police commissioner was also infamous for his use of brutality against civil rights demonstrators and black people as a whole.

In 1963, Birmingham had never had a single black police officer or firefighter. Most of the black citizens were not enrolled to vote, and bombings of black properties occurred so often they were commonplace.

In the previous eight years, the city had experienced twenty-one separate bombings at churches and other properties owned and linked to black citizens. These bombings became so common that the city was nicknamed 'Bombingham'.

Because of its reputation as one of the strongholds of white supremacy, Birmingham attracted more attention from those involved in the Civil Rights Movement, and became a particular focus in the efforts to end segregation in the Deep South.

Just a few years earlier, Martin Luther King Jr. had been arrested in Birmingham while leading supporters in a demonstration. As a result of this arrest, and his subsequent time in jail, he wrote the famous 'Letter From a Birmingham Jail', confirming his decision to not cease the demonstrations, regardless of the bloodshed from local law enforcement. The letter was published in newspapers nationally, along with images of police brutality against protestors.

During the 1960's the 16th Street Baptist Church in Birmingham was a fundamental part of the Civil Rights Movement in the city. It was the place where many activist meetings were held, and the church had also served as a meeting place for the city's African American community.

It was where students arrested in the 1963 Birmingham movement had been trained and organized by the Southern Christian Leadership Conference (SCLC). As well as Martin Luther King, the church had also been used as a meeting place for Ralph David Abernathy and Fred Shuttlesworth. The SCLC had also been part of a campaign to help Birmingham's African American citizens register to vote.

As well as services and civil rights meetings, the church was also used as a social center and also as a lecture hall. It was well known as an important location to the black community of Birmingham, so much so that the KKK routinely called in bomb threats to the church, trying to disrupt both civil rights meetings and regular church services and events.

On The Day In Question:
Midmorning on Sunday, September 15th, 1964, the peace was shattered at the 16th Street Baptist Church. At 10:22am, the church was full. Around two hundred members were at the church, joining in activities before the 11:00am service. Children were attending Sunday School and there was also a group of children changing into their choir robes in the basement.

The church's phone rang and the acting Sunday School secretary, Carolyn Maull, answered. Maull herself was just fourteen years old. The caller said just two words to her—"two minutes"—and then hung up.

Under a minute later, before Maull even had time to work out what the caller was talking about, the ground shook. A bomb detonated on the east side of the church, throwing bricks from the front of the structure and causing internal walls to cave in.

Most of the congregation managed to escape the building, but not altogether unscathed. Over twenty were injured in the blast.

Tragically it was discovered that four young girls—Addie Mae Collins (14), Cynthia Wesley (14), Carole Robertson (14) and Denise McNair (11)—had not escaped. The girls' bodies were found lying beneath rubble in a basement bathroom.

The power of the blast had been so immense that the force of the explosion decapitated one girl. Her body was so badly disfigured that her clothing was used to identify her. Another of the girls had died when brick mortar embedded itself in her head. The girls were found still clinging to each other. Another girl in the same room, Sarah Collins (10), Addie Mae's sister, had survived the building collapse, but lost her right eye in the explosion.

A survivor would later say that the explosion had shaken the whole church. It blew a seven-foot diameter hole in a rear wall of the church, and formed a five-foot crater in the basement. The shockwave also propelled a passing driver completely outside of his car, and destroyed more cars parked nearby.

The blast was so powerful that properties more than two blocks away from the church sustained damage. At the church, only one stained glass window survived the blast, a mural of Jesus with a group of small children.

Despite the political unrest in Birmingham at the time, the church congregation was not without help. Hundreds of people, including those wounded by the explosion, started to search for survivors in the debris even as police put up barriers surrounding the church.

It's estimated that at one stage, more than two thousand black people surrounded the church, Reverend John Cross reading the 23rd Psalm to the crowd with a bullhorn. Several people noticed a sole white man standing at the barricade, watching the fire.

It was long before people began reacting to the shocking blast. Within hours, violence was escalating throughout the city. Police began urging both white and black families to stay off the streets. Governor Wallace ordered in an extra three hundred State Police, and the City Council called an emergency meeting, trying to deal with city safety issues and potential increased civil unrest.

Despite these efforts, within twenty-four hours after the church bombing, firebombs were set off in at least five local properties and cars, mostly driven by white drivers, were stoned by rioters.

Some groups did glorify the death of black children, particularly white supremacist groups, but on the whole the reaction from both black and whites was one of horror and that until now the Civil Rights Movement had not been given enough attention.

A young white man, Charles Morgan Jr., who was a lawyer, spoke to a group of businessmen in Birmingham, saying that every person who had ever engaged in a racist comment or action, however small, had contributed to the bombing of the church.

The bombing was the end of the violence towards blacks that day. Within seven hours of the bombing, two black teenagers, Johnny Robinson (16) and Virgil Ware (13) were shot and killed in Birmingham. Robinson was shot in the back while running away from police.

Police had arrived in the area after reports of black boys throwing stones at cars, and Robinson did not stop running when ordered to. Ware was shot by another young man who was returning with a friend from a rally against integration. There seemed to be absolutely no provocation from Ware.

Investigation:

The start of investigations into the bombing was swift. Birmingham Mayor Albert Boutwell condemned the bombings as "just sickening", and the Attorney General sent twenty-five FBI agents to the city to assist with the forensic investigation, including explosive experts.

Shortly after the bombing, a white man was seen driving through the area flying a Confederate flag. The police took him into custody.

Investigators initially worked on the assumption that someone had thrown a bomb from a car as it drove past. By September 20th the FBI agents had confirmed that instead a bomb had been purposely planted on the building itself, beneath the church steps.

The investigation quickly focused on a local group who had splintered off from the KKK, the Cahaba Boys. They had formed their own group earlier that year, believing that the KKK was becoming impotent in their defense of white supremacy.

The group had been mentioned in relation to several earlier bombings of homes of community leaders and business owners in the black community. While the group was small, it had some notable members, including Thomas Blanton Jr., Robert Chambliss, Herman Frank Cash, and Bobby Cherry.

Multiple witness statements reported seeing white men near the church the morning of the bombing in a turquoise 1957 Chevrolet. Some witnesses saw a white man leave the car and approach the church steps where the bomb had been found. Descriptions of the man varied. Both Chambliss and Cherry were potential matches.

The city of Birmingham offered a $52,000 reward for the arrest of those responsible. Governor Wallace himself added an addition $5000 to the reward on behalf of the State of Alabama. While his contribution was accepted, he was not seen to be without guilt himself. Dr. Martin Luther King Jr. sent Wallace a telegram, saying that "the blood of four little children" was on his hands.

The FBI brought Chambliss in for questioning on the 26th of September, but it did not bring the justice that many sought. Three days later he was indicted for illegally purchasing and transporting dynamite only.

He, along with acquaintances Charles Cagle and John Hall, was convicted on October 8th of illegally possessing and transporting dynamite. They each received a wholly suspended jail term of 180 days, and were fined just $100. No charges of murder, Federal or otherwise, were brought against any of the men. Formally, the bombing was an open, unsolved case.

The FBI said years later that they had four serious suspects in the case of the bombing, including four members of the splinter group—Blanton, Cash, Chambliss, and Cherry. However, many witnesses were wary about speaking out against the men, and there was little physical evidence in the case.

In 1965, the FBI along with local investigators formally named Blanton, Cash, Chambliss, and Cherry as the perpetrators. The believed Chambliss was the ringleader. The information made it all the way to the top to J. Edgar Hoover, the Director of the FBI. However, based on reported mistrust between Federal and local investigators, once again no prosecutions ever took place.

Later in 1965, Hoover went so far as to formally block any prosecutions against the four men, and refused to release any evidence the FBI had with either Federal or State prosecutors. The FBI closed the investigation without filing any charges in 1968, and Hoover ordered the files sealed.

Meanwhile, as a result of the church bombing, more focus was now on the Civil Rights Movement as a whole. Events such as the March on Washington, and the assassination of President John F. Kennedy, a strong supporter of civil rights, increased worldwide support for the movement.

Following Kennedy's death, the new president Lyndon Johnson signed the Civil Rights Act of 1964 into effect. Officially however, the bombing of the 16th Street Church remained unsolved.

In 1971 William Baxley was elected as Alabama's Attorney General. He had been a student at university when the bombings took place, and reported that he always felt he wanted to do something about it, but hadn't known what.

Within a week of being sworn into office, Baxley had combed through the original police investigation reports, finding them lackluster and inefficient. Not put off, he formally reopened the case.

This time, Baxley himself was able to find key witnesses who had been reluctant to testify the first time around, and build a trust between them. Other witnesses were able to place Chambliss definitively as the person who had placed the bomb beneath the church's steps.

Baxley found evidence that proved Chambliss had bought dynamite from a store less than two weeks before the bombing. He was also able to place Chambliss' car in the area on the day of the bombing.

Baxley requested and was granted access to the original FBI files. He discovered evidence against the four named suspects, including Chambliss, which had previously not been released to anyone else.

Although he met with some initial resistance from the FBI, after he threatened to expose the Department of Justice for withholding evidence, Baxley was given access.

Finally, on September 24th, 1977, fourteen years after the bombing, Chambliss was indicted for four counts of murder. He went to trial on November 14th. He was seventy-three years old when the trial began.

Despite Chambliss' indictment, at the initial hearing on October 18th, Judge Wallace Gibson ruled that he would stand trial for only one murder—McNair's, the youngest victim—the other counts would remain, but Chambliss would not be tried for them.

Chambliss, who was released on a $200,000 bond before the trial, pleaded not guilty. He blamed another KKK member, Gary Thomas Rowe, Jr. as the one who actually set the bomb, claiming he only bought the dynamite.

Two law enforcement officers testified for the prosecution against Chambliss' claim of innocence. One was a retired Birmingham police officer, Tom Cook, who testified that Chambliss had admitted he bought the dynamite in 1975, but had told him that he had given the dynamite to Rowe.

Ernie Cantrell, a police sergeant at the time, testified that in 1975 Chambliss had told him that another member of the KKK had been entirely responsible. He also testified that Chambliss had boasted about his bomb making knowledge to him.

On cross-examination, Cantrell said that Chambliss had also denied to him he was a part of the bombing, but why had he blamed two different people as the actual perpetrator within the one year?

Another KKK member also testified against Chambliss, saying that Chambliss had been frustrated the organization was dragging its feet on protesting racial integration.

Perhaps one of the most crucial witnesses for the prosecution was someone very close to Chambliss—his own niece, Reverend Elizabeth Cobbs. She testified that her uncle had told her repeatedly that he was engaged in a 'one man battle' with blacks since the 1940's.

She told the court that the day before the bombing, Chambliss had told her he had enough dynamite to flatten half of the city. She also testified that a week after the bombing, she had been watching a news report with Chambliss about the girls who died. He allegedly told her that the bomb wasn't meant to hurt anyone, and that it hadn't gone off when it was supposed to.

In his closing arguments, Baxley would acknowledge that Chambliss was not the sole guilty party in the bombing. He also expressed regret that he could not ask for the death penalty, as it currently only applied to crimes committed after its reinstatement from an earlier repeal of the law.

The defense argued that the evidence against Chambliss was purely circumstantial, and was similar to the evidence that had acquitted Chambliss back in 1963. During the trial, they also called twelve different witnesses who testified that Chambliss had been elsewhere on the day of the bombing, including testimony from a police officer.

The jury deliberated for more than six hours, and the next day, on November 18th, 1977, Chambliss was found guilty of murder. He received a life sentence, all while still protesting his innocence.

Current Status:
The boy who shot Virgil Ware and his friend were both convicted of second-degree manslaughter. A judge later suspended their sentences, and gave them just two years probation.

On the same afternoon that Chambliss was found guilty, Baxley issued a subpoena to Blanton, attempting to scare him into confessing his own involvement in the bombing. However, Blanton just hired a lawyer, and refused to answer any of Baxley's questions.

Chambliss appealed his conviction. He again claimed that the evidence against him was entirely circumstantial, and that the fourteen-year gap between the crime and his trial had violated his right to a speedy trial, saying the delay was a tactic used by the prosecution to gain an advantage. However on May 22nd, 1979 his appeal was dismissed.

Chambliss died in the hospital in 1985, eight years after his conviction. He had spent those eight years in solitary to protect him from fellow inmates. To the day he died, he insisted that Rowe had been the one to set the bomb.

Chambliss' death was not the end of the case. Ten years after he died, the FBI re-opened their own investigation using evidence they had gathered in the 1960's that they had not made available to Blaxley.

In early May of 2000, the FBI announced that they had found that the bombing had been carried out by four members of the

KKK, known as the Cahaba Boys. They were Blanton, Cash, Chambliss, and Cherry. Cash had also since died, but Blanton and Cherry were both arrested.

They were indicted with four counts of first-degree murder and four counts of universal malice on May 16th, 2000. Cherry's trial was postponed indefinitely due to a finding that dementia had impaired his mind to the point he could not assist with his own defense.

Due to Cherry's trial postponement, Blanton stood alone at his own trial. His trial began on April 24th, 2001, and he pleaded not guilty. The prosecution called seven witnesses, including relatives of the victims, an FBI agent, and a former KKK member who had become a paid FBI informant.

The most damning evidence presented at trial was a secret recording taken by the FBI in 1964, in which Blanton was discussing his involvement in the bombing with his wife. His wife had accused him of having an affair, and he told her that he was not at the other woman's house, but instead at a meeting to plan a bombing.

The defense argued that the tape had been edited by the FBI and spliced a longer conversation together, also attacking its audio quality. Recordings were also presented between Blanton and the paid informant, but they were portrayed as 'two rednecks' making false claims.

The defense emphasized that the informant had earlier testified that Blanton had never expressly said he had made or placed the bomb. The defense called only two witnesses themselves, one who testified he had seen Blanton elsewhere at the time of the bombing.

Despite it now being thirty-eight years since the bombing occurred Blanton was found guilty of four counts of first-degree murder after just two and a half hours of deliberation by the jury. Blanton was sentenced to life in prison. He is the sole perpetrator who is still alive today.

In January 2002 a judge found Cherry competent to stand trial. Again, it was argued that the evidence was circumstantial. Willadean Brogdon, Cherry's ex-wife, testified that Cherry had boasted that he had been the one to plant the bomb at the church's steps, and also the one that lit the fuse hours later.

That would explain why there was no timer found in the debris after the bombing. Many of the same audiotapes from Blanton's trial were used again at Cherry's. This time the judge ruled that some sections were too prejudicial, and only some could be used as evidence.

After almost seven hours of deliberation, on May 22nd, 2002, Cherry was also found guilty of four counts of first-degree murder. He too was sentenced to life in prison. He died of cancer on November 18th, 2004.

Rowe, the man accused by Chambliss of setting the bomb, became a paid FBI informant just two months after the bombing. He had a long history of violence against blacks.

Although Rowe was never formally named by law enforcement of being involved, he did fail two separate polygraph tests when questioned about his involvement in the bombings. Despite a 1979 investigation clearing Rowe, perhaps Chambliss' claims did hold some truth?

In the months after the bombing, the 16th Street Baptist Church received over $186,000 in donations from members and the wider public, from all around the world. The church was rebuilt and continues to be a place of worship today, with services attracting up to 2,000 people.

On May 24th, 2013, President Barack Obama posthumously awarded the Congressional Gold Medal to the four victims killed in the bombing. The medal was presented to the Birmingham Civil Rights Institute.

The bombing continues to be featured in multiple feature films, TV shows, books, and artworks.

Victim: Leslie Long
Date: December 3rd, 1978
Location: Palmdale, Los Angeles
Suspects: Neal Matthews and Terry Moses and two unnamed prison escapees

Backstory:
Leslie Long was a twenty year-old mother of three who lived in Palmdale, Los Angeles County, California. Married to her high school sweetheart, they had three children; two girls aged four and three, and a baby son.

Long and her husband had married when Long was just fifteen years old. They had eloped together to Las Vegas. Long had completed her high school equivalency course, and wanted to become a registered nurse. She had lived in Palmdale all her life.

Long worked as a gas station attendant at a Chevron station, and had told her family she was proud to be working a man's job. She had taken the job to pay for new furniture for her house and to buy Christmas presents for her family.

Long was usually a last minute shopper, but according to her sister Patsy Long, that year she had already picked out everyone's presents early. Most of the purchases were on layaway, and some were already gift-wrapped.

Long and her sister had married brothers, and in the spring or summer of 1978, Long suddenly asked her sister whether she would take care of her children, should anything happen to her. She promised, and asked Long to do the same for her. Patsy tragically honored her promise much sooner than she ever suspected.

On The Day In Question:
On Sunday December 3rd, 1978, Long was working alone at the gas station. She was working the closing shift when two men entered and attempted to rob the store. The two men first stole money from the safe in the store, before forcing Long into a car at gunpoint and kidnapping her.

Another customer arrived at the store at 9:30pm and found the store's office door wide open, the lights all still on, but no staff present. The customer found the safe open but empty, and coins scattered across the floor. A woman's purse was still in the office and an empty car parked in the lot at the back of the store. The customer called the authorities.

Antelope Valley Sheriff Deputies quickly responded, and a massive manhunt was begun for Long, but nothing was found. Three days later on Wednesday, December 6th, a plane participating in a search by air spotted a body lying at the base of a hill just off Freeway 14 in Acton, just eight miles south of the gas station where Long worked.

Investigators from the Sheriff's Homicide unit responded and found Long's body. She was still wearing her uniform from work. Long had been shot, and had died at the scene. It was later revealed at autopsy that she had been raped.

Investigation:
Early evidence from the crime scenes revealed that there were at least two perpetrators involved in the kidnapping, rape, and murder of Long.

The crime attracted a large amount of attention from the media, and suspicion quickly fell on two prisoners who had escaped from a prison in Northern California just three days before Long's murder.

One of the men had been convicted just a year earlier of robbing a gas station, kidnapping the attendant, taking him to a remote location and then killing him with a shot to the head. It was not hard to believe that he had struck again in an extremely similar case.

The prisoners were found and recaptured, but there was not enough evidence to charge them with any crime related to Long. Although public sentiment was that they were definitely involved in her rape and murder, no charges were made and the case went cold. At least though, thought Long's family, some comfort could be taken from the fact that the accused men where back behind bars for their earlier crimes.

Time passed, and detectives opened the Long file in an attempt to solve the case, but then left it again, unsolved. Although the case was officially classified as a cold case, prosecutors have said that there was always one detective quietly investigating.

Meanwhile, DNA technology advanced way beyond anything dreamed of in 1978. DNA from Long's case was re-run after new leads and tips of a person of interest was sent to the Sheriff.

Two samples were available from the crime scene, but originally only one could be tested, the other degraded past the point of analysis. In 2011 a new technology called MiniFiler, which amplifies the sample, advanced to the point that the second sample could now also be tested.

Los Angeles County Sheriff's Sgt. Brian Schoonmaker arranged for both samples to be tested against the escaped prisoner suspects in an attempt to close the case once and for all. Instead, to most people's surprise a match was not found. In fact the DNA was reportedly not even close to that of the escaped prisoners. They had never been involved.

Thirty-three years after Long's murder, Schoonmaker reported that with the escapees cleared as suspects, the investigation was "…back to, basically, square one."

The Board of Supervisors, a government body that oversees the operation of all county government in California (along with other states), authorized a $20,000 reward for information identifying Long's killers.

Both the gas company where Long worked and the city of Palmdale had already offered smaller rewards of $5,000 and $1,000, respectively. Along with the new higher reward amount offered, in October 2001 the television show Crime Stoppers aired a reenactment of the case.

Schoonmaker hoped that the screening would trigger a memory for a witness, or help to develop further leads in the case. Long's children, now adults in their thirties, were hopeful that the show would help someone step forward. With a DNA sample now available to compare to, hopefully identifying the killer would be an easier task.

The show aired, but nothing significant came from the investigation, and Long's murder remained unsolved.

Time passed, and a detective named Steven Lankford took over the case from Schoonmaker. In 2015 the case broke wide open. The DNA was tested again with more advanced technology, and this time a match was found.

Sperm belonging to two men, Neal Matthews and Terry Moses, was found in samples taken from Long's body. Matthews, from Lancaster and now fifty-eight years old, was arrested on May 21st, 2015 for murder. He appeared in court on May 26th, 2015, where he did not enter a plea.

Matthews was held without bail. On the same day the L.A. County District Attorney's office filed a warrant for the arrest of Terry Moses, fifty-nine, for murder. Moses was currently serving a life sentence for an unrelated case as a three-strikes inmate convicted for multiple robberies, his first committed when he was still a juvenile. He is scheduled to appear before the court for Long's murder at a later date.

Because Long had been killed while in the process of another felony (both the robbery and the kidnapping) the case could potentially be tried as a capital murder case, bringing the death penalty into consideration.

It was discovered by investigators that at the time of Long's murder, both suspects had been active gang members.

Current Status:
At the time of this writing, Matthews is scheduled to be arraigned on felony murder charges on June 16th, 2015. Prosecutors have yet to announce whether they intend to seek the death penalty.

The original suspect, exonerated with DNA evidence, remains in prison, serving a life sentence for an unrelated murder.

His fellow escapee was released from prison, but then died in a motorcycle accident in 1982, just one year after he was paroled. DNA from his mother and brother were used to prove his innocence posthumously in Long's rape and murder.

At the time of Long's death, her mother told the media that her children had not taken her death well. In particular, Christy, who was the eldest at nearly five years old, completely withdrew. Jimmy, who was a baby at the time, continually called out for his mother.

Patsy Long kept her promise to her sister. When Leslie Long's husband died in 1980 in a motorcycle accident, just eighteen months after Long's death, Pasty and her husband Mark took their three children under their wing and raised them along with four children of their own.

At the same time as being charged with Long's kidnapping and murder, Moses was charged with killing Carlton Goodwin and Michael Fuqua in 1976, and the attempted murder of Kenney Guevara in 1996. Police continue to ask anyone with information regarding the case to contact the L.A. County Sheriff's Department.

Victim: Outlaw Motorcycle Club Murders
Date: July 4th, 1979
Location: Charlotte, North Carolina
Suspects: Hells Angels motorcycle club members, and Gregory Scott Lindamann and Randy Allen Pigg

Backstory:
The Outlaw Motorcycle Club, incorporated as the American Outlaws Association (AOA) was founded in McCook, Illinois in 1935. They are a one-percenter club. This term originated from a comment by the American Motorcyclist Association that 99% of motorcyclists were law-abiding citizens.

Being a one-percenter club identifies the club as an outlaw club. Some clubs have gone so far as to wear a 1% patch on their vest as a badge of honor, or to instill fear and respect from other motorcyclists and members of the general public.

On the flip side, some members of the outlaw clubs point out that many of the groups are also involved in charitable causes, and that a few bad members does not a criminal organization make.

Membership in the AOA is restricted to men who own American-made motorcycles of a particular size. Some branches in Europe allow bikes from any country as long as they are of a particular style. The main rival club of the Outlaws is the Hells Angels, another well-known one-percenter club.

In the 1970's, Charlotte, North Carolina, was a major southern hub for multiple bandit motorcycle gangs, including the Outlaws. Criminal rackets such as prostitution rings and drug deals were run through the clubs. Charlotte was halfway between the chemists in Canada and the prime drug market in Miami, and was used as a key station in the drug trafficking pipeline.

The AOA meanwhile had set up a fortress in a rented house on Allen Road South, Charlotte. The house was surrounded by eight-foot fences, and had multiple vicious dogs guarding the property.

On The Day In Question:
Early in the morning of July 4th, 1979, Outlaw leader William 'Chains' Flamont arrived at the clubhouse, and discovered something he could not have imagined. A probationary member of the club, William 'Water Head' Allen, just twenty-two years of age, was found dead on the porch. His body was riddled with bullets and was found still leaning back in his chair. His .38 caliber pistol lay in his lap.

Flamont then found a second member just inside the door, also dead. William 'Mouse' Dronenburg (32) lay sprawled on the floor with his legs wrapped in a blanket from the couch. He too had a gun lying near his body. It had not been fired.

On the couch was seventeen-year old Bridgette 'Midget' Benfield. She had run away from home after becoming involved with the biker culture a few months earlier. She had been shot in the head and was also dead.

Behind Benfield was the body of Leonard 'Terrible Terry' Henderson (29). He too was near an unfired gun.

Finally, on another couch lay Randall Feazell (28), with his body covered in bullet holes from his leg to his face. He was not a member of the Outlaws.

Sometime on Independence Day 1979, someone had scaled the eight-foot fence, avoided the guard dogs, and killed five people involved with a one-percent motorcycle club.

Investigation:
Autopsies showed that none of the victims had a single trace of drugs or alcohol in their bodies at the time of death. Investigators believed that time of death was around midnight the night before, and that the victims had likely been killed in their sleep. Police estimated that the entire attack was over in just fifteen seconds.

The victim's bodies were riddled with so many bullets that the medical examiner stopped counting. Police recovered over thirty shell casings from the clubhouse floor.

The immediate response was that a rival outlaw gang must have been responsible, suspicion falling on the Hells Angels. At the time of the killings they were involved in a territorial dispute with the Outlaws.

The use of Charlotte by multiple motorcycle clubs as part of the national network to distribute drugs and undertake other criminal activities had created a war between the different clubs.

Investigators report that finding anyone willing to testify against members of any club was extremely difficult. Therefore, the FBI decided to send in an undercover agent who already rode a motorcycle, Agent Lance Emery. The investigation was codenamed Operation Counterveil.

Using the alias Alan Ray Price, Emery started to attempt to infiltrate the local bike gangs. He introduced himself as a fence for stolen property who was trying to move into the drug business. Drug trafficking was a major source of income for the Outlaw club.

His prime target was the president of the Outlaws, a major player in the drug trade. His name was Flamont, the man who discovered the bodies at the house. Emery remained undercover for months, gathering evidence of their activities and sending it to his handler.

He developed a friendship with a stripper, Pam Little, who was becoming disenfranchised with the life of a biker. Emery revealed his true identity to her, and asked her to introduce him to those she knew, giving credibility to Emery's fake identity.

Offered help with her son, who was in trouble with law enforcement, Little agreed and with her help the investigation stepped up to the next level. She introduced Emery to several key contacts, and also helped with the setup of a house that they bugged with audio and video equipment. FBI agents set themselves up four houses down, and tracked all illegal activity occurring in the house.

Eventually, tension between the Hells Angels and Outlaws reached the boiling point, and two further bikers were murdered, one being the president of the Hells Angels in Charlotte.

A member of the Outlaws and friend of Little's named Shortcut was then injured in an attempt to blow up the Hells Angels clubhouse. Still attempting to get in good with the Outlaws president 'Chains' Flamont, Emery took over the care of Shortcut while he was recovering. Emery was starting to become discouraged as to his progress while undercover. He'd been in deep cover for months, and had barely seen his wife.

Meanwhile, surveillance on the clubhouse revealed Snowman, a man from Detroit, who had connections with Flamont. Emery tried to use Little to setup a meeting with Snowman. Pam assured Emery that a deal would go down with no problems, and so Emery traveled to Detroit.

When he got there however, he was threatened with a gun and his identity questioned. Snowman called Flamont, who vouched for Emery's undercover alter identity. His hard work had paid off. On Emery's return, Flamont told him that he'd returned the favor after Emery looked after Shortcut, and that next time he wanted to do business, he didn't have to travel all the way to Detroit.

Emery stayed undercover, and he and Flamont became friendly. He visited Emery at the house often, and participated in several drug deals, all while being monitored by the FBI. Despite this, Emery was growing tired.

By this time, he'd been undercover for eighteen months. After reviewing everything they'd accomplished, and the ongoing danger to Emery, the FBI decided to pull him and close the investigation. The FBI, along with other law enforcement agencies, arrested fourteen gang members, including Flamont.

They also arrested Emery to protect his cover, and he was quickly released afterwards. In separate raids over the summer Hells Angels members were arrested also, leaving only a handful of members in each chapter in North Carolina.

Despite the arrests, the exact identity of the murderers remained unknown. Law enforcement continued investigating, never moving the case to cold cases, despite its age. Two men, Gregory Scott Lindamann and Randy Allen Pigg, were named as official persons of interest in the case.

Neither of the men were members of a motorcycle gang, but they did have personal ties to one of the victims. Lindamann had been arrested on an unrelated murder warrant in California in July 1979, and was returned to Charlotte for questioning regarding the clubhouse murders. Police also found Pigg locally and interviewed him. Despite the investigation, the pair was never arrested, police citing lack of evidence. Despite not belonging to a club, the men's reputations were far from clean, and many were afraid to testify against them. It was a very long time before anyone would.

In July 2015, Charlotte-Mecklenburg police announced that they had identified the people responsible for the Outlaw clubhouse murders, over three decades since the fateful night.

Police had continued to investigate through the decades, and now say they had enough evidence to see the full picture. They still could not arrest anyone for the murders. This time, it was because both of the named members were dead.

Lindamann had died in a car accident in Texas on October 15th, 1990. Meanwhile, Pigg, who had suffered from multiple medical conditions, had died of liver failure on October 5th, 2007.

Police officially closed the case of the Outlaw Clubhouse murders on Wednesday, July 8th, 2015.

Current Status:
Emery has said in hindsight that he would not go undercover again. He believes he was lucky that time, and isn't so sure he'd come out alive again. The arrests tied to his work broke up the Outlaw's meth network, which had supplied the entire state.

Emery's investigation was followed by Operation Rough Rider, another investigation which lead to the arrest of outlaw bikers all over the USA. Before Operation Counterveil there had been little systematic effort to investigate biker gangs, despite multiple previous murders linked to the gangs in Charlotte.

The first investigator of the murders, Ron Guerette, believed that the deaths were a wake-up call to Charlotte, and started the sharing of information regarding biker chapters between different law enforcement agencies and states for the first time.

Hundreds of members of the Outlaws from chapters around the country rode into Charlotte for the funerals of the slain members. The club continues to have a presence in Charlotte to this day.

In an interesting twist to the case, although he was never considered a suspect, Flamont's own gun was considered the probable murder weapon. He had left it at the house the night before the murders, and it had now vanished.

Flamont, now 52, says he retired from the Outlaws after the murders, and now lives near Gastonia, North Carolina with his wife. He works as a technician at Harley-Davidson Inc.

Victim: Janet Robinson
Date: May 15th, 1987
Location: Fernandina Beach, Florida
Suspects: James Lee Hall Jr., Robert Way and Octavian Brewton

Backstory:
Janet Robinson (nee Simmons) was among the first students to attend the new Peck School in Nassau County, Florida in 1936. The school was closed at the end of segregation in the county, and Robinson was part of the last graduating class. She was a talented singer, and her yearbook indicates that she planned a career in Gospel music. Her classmates, including a future Fernandina Beach mayor, voted her 'Most Popular'.

Robinson met Jeremiah 'Jerry' Mattox and married him at First Missionary Baptist Church in Fernandina Beach in 1950. He had moved there from Georgia in 1950 after a Nassau County Sheriff convinced him to take a position as the first black deputy in the county. He was looking for someone to patrol American Beach. A white deputy had been severely injured by two black men at that location.

Just four years later, Mattox suffered worse. He became the first black police officer to be killed in the line of duty. He was shot while trying to arrest a man for domestic violence. Robinson was on her way home from the beach when the incident occurred, and some reports say that she witnessed her husband's death.

A couple of years later she married again, but the marriage failed and Robinson moved to Cleveland, Ohio. Sometime around 1984, she moved back to Fernandina Beach and was employed as a cook at a local restaurant.

On The Day In Question:
On May 15th, 1987, Robinson, then fifty-six years old, was found dead in her home. Robinson had been raped and then strangled. Friends and neighbors told police that Robinson rarely allowed anyone to come inside her house.

Investigators believed that the killer had entered the home uninvited through an unlocked back door, possibly earlier in the evening before or the morning that Robinson's body was found.

The crime scene revealed that Robinson had been attacked forcefully, the killer attempting to pin her to the floor. Had he meant to kill her, or had she been strangled in an attempt to subdue her and overcome her resistance to a robbery?

Foreign DNA was found on Robinson's body, but no match was found in CODIS.

Investigation:
A witness reported that they had seen James Lee Hall Jr. running from the crime scene. Hall had a criminal past, having been arrested for sexually assaulting his mother's best friend six months prior. Police reported that Hall's mother had talked her friend into dropping the complaint, and so no charges were ever brought, nor were any DNA samples taken from Hall.

Hall had known Robinson, and had helped her out with projects around the house prior to her murder. He would have known the layout of the inside of her home.

Police arrested Hall, but then Robert Way came forward and told police that the real perpetrator had been Octavian Brewton, with Way acting as a look out. Both men were subsequently arrested, and the police let Hall go.

After this, Way failed a polygraph test, and then admitted to police that he'd made the whole thing up. Brewton was not charged. Way was sentenced to six months jail for providing false information on a crime.

Investigators discovered that Brewton had a shady alibi for that night. He had been committing burglary that same night in another town. Still, both he and Way's DNA were tested against the sample found on Robinson's body. No match was found, and they were both ruled out as suspects. Brewton now remained in custody due to the burglary charge.

Meanwhile, Hall moved to Colorado just months after Robinson's murder. For whatever reason, detectives working the case never turned their attentions back to him. Time passed, and the case went cold.

Over the years, several investigators tried to solve the case, but due to lack of resources were never able to devote enough time to the case. Fernandina Beach Police Chief James Hurley convinced former Police Captain Jim Coe to come out of retirement to work on the case.

Coe had originally worked the case, and then handed it to someone else when he retired. He had over thirty years of law enforcement experience behind him, and was invited back to mentor new detectives and renew focus on Robinson's murder investigation.

Coe's investigation led him back to James Hall Jr. He became suspicious when he found discrepancies in what Hall had told police regarding when he had last seen Robinson and also when he had been at her house both on and prior to the night she was murdered.

Hall had originally told police that he'd seen Robinson at a liquor store around 5:00pm on the night she'd been killed. That made him one of the last people to see her alive. His statements to police regarding his activities after seeing Robinson at the store that night contradicted other statements he'd made when discussing his alibi.

He initially said that he'd never gone to Robinson's home, but then later told police that he'd eaten lunch at Robinson's house once after helping her hang some blinds. It appears that this lunch may have taken place just a week before she was killed.

His statements also contradicted the reports of his own activities that night. He told police that after he'd seen Robinson at the store he had gone home and stayed there for the rest of the night.

He later said that he'd gone to a neighbor's house to help him paint around 6:00-7:00pm. He then said that after painting he'd gone to a local bar around 11:00pm, where he'd stayed until 1:00am.

The neighbor that he helped paint said that he'd seen Hall at another friend's house later that night. Hall hadn't mentioned this friend in any interviews with police.

Coe also found the woman who had reportedly seen Hall running away from Robinson's house the night she was killed and re-interviewed her in 2011. It had been nearly twenty-five years since the murder, but she had not changed her story.

She told Coe that she'd seen Hall fleeing the scene around 3:00 or 4:00am. She reported that Hall had been sweating profusely and appeared to be running from something.

Coe looked into Hall's background, and found a pattern of criminal activity. His crimes included trespassing, domestic violence, burglary, and at least one sexual battery. His activities spanned across three states; Florida, Kansas, and Colorado.

His crimes in Fernandina Beach followed the same pattern, all involving an older woman who lived alone. They were also all friends of his mother, who he lived with at the time. The assaults were all near his home, and all occurred either late at night or early in the morning.

Coe believed that Hall befriended these women, doing odd jobs and helping out around their homes. This likely gained him easy access to their houses. Coe also believed that Hall was betting on the victim's relationship with his mother making it less likely that the women would report him for his crimes.

However, Coe could no longer question Hall himself. Hall had died in Colorado in 2000. He was a U.S. Air Force veteran, and had been buried in Fort Logan National Cemetery after dying of natural causes. Despite his prior criminal activity, a DNA sample had never been taken from Hall. Coe approached Hall's family, but they refused to co-operate with police or give a DNA sample.

Coe approached a judge, and ultimately drew up a probable cause warrant requesting that Hall's body be exhumed for DNA testing. A judge agreed and in December 2014 Hall's remains were exhumed and tissue samples removed. The Florida Department of Law Enforcement tested the samples against the sample from Robinson's body taken in 1987, and a match was found.

The murder of Janet Robinson had been solved, but it was a bittersweet moment. Nearly thirty years after her death, Robinson had no known surviving family members to hear the news her killer had been found.

Robinson's case was solved during Black History Month, a gratifying end given Robinson's history with Peck High School and the manner of her first husband's death.

Current Status:

Jim Coe believes that it is highly likely that family members coerced Hall's mother's friend into dropping the charges against him. He has said that had those people not interfered then, DNA would likely have been taken and Robinson may well still be alive today.

Police are now comparing Hall's DNA sample to open sexual assault cases in Colorado, Kansas and Florida, to see if any more cases are linked to Hall.

Victim: Mary Jayne Jones
Date: April 9th, 1974
Location: Ottumwa, Iowa
Suspect: Robert Pilcher

Backstory:
Mary Jayne Jones was born on September 10th, 1956. She lived in Ottumwa, Iowa. Jones had grown up in Fayetteville, North Carolina, and had recently moved to Ottumwa just nine months earlier to help her sister, Pat, who was expecting a baby.

The baby had been born in November and Pat had returned to Fayetteville. Jones however decided to stay in Iowa. She had a job, new friends, and her own apartment and didn't want to leave. She was seventeen years old.

Jones was a short young woman, standing at 5'2", and had auburn hair. Friends described her as outgoing. Jones was friends with fellow employees at her job, who described her as bubbly and a super girl.

Her other sister Judith described Jones as an amazing individual. She told the media that Jones was always happy and full of life. She had strong family values, and would always help someone else if she could.

While she did not have any particular career aspirations at seventeen years old, Judith is sure that Jones would have ended up working in a profession where she could help other people.

According to fellow employees at the drive-in where Jones worked, her good looks and happy personality attracted attention from some of the male customers. One man, Robert Pilcher was known for making unwanted and sometimes lewd advances towards the waitresses.

Pilcher was much older than Jones at twenty-seven, and owned an extermination business. He approached Jones more than once, nagging her for a date. However, no one remembers her ever saying yes.

One night everything changed. Jones' youngest sister Judith remembers a phone call in the middle of the night on April 9th back at their home in North Carolina. Her mother answered, and Judith heard only her mother screaming uncontrollably. Her older sister had been murdered.

On The Day In Question:
Very little is known about Jones' activities that day. Her boyfriend, Ron Nichols testified that he stopped by the restaurant where Jones worked on April 9th around noon to see her. She was last seen at a bank in town.

On Tuesday April 9th, 1974 Jones' body was found in a farmhouse near Blakesburg, Iowa approximately seven miles from Ottumwa. She was naked and lying on a bed.

Investigation:
The first police knew of Jones' murder was when they received a phone call around 5:00pm on April 9th, 1975. Ernest Marlin called the Wapello County sheriff's office and told police that his wife had discovered the body of a young woman in a farmhouse.

Ernest Marlin worked at the farm owned by his son Max Marlin. He had been working at the farm that day, but Jones' body was not discovered until his wife came to bring him dinner that afternoon. She had been the one to find Jones' body in the farmhouse bedroom.

Early investigations discovered that Max Marlin was away on vacation in California at the time that Jones had been killed. Police believed that the farmhouse had been unoccupied when she had been killed, although the elder Marlins had stayed at the farm a couple of nights before.

Jones had been sexually assaulted, and then killed by close range shots to the head and to the heart. She had been shot only twice by a high-powered rifle. There was no frenzied shooting, the killing cold and methodical. There were no other injuries on the body, nor were any defensive wounds present that would indicate a struggle.

Multiple guns were found in the farmhouse, but they were not checked to determine if any of them was the murder weapon. The crime lab did process the scene along with local law enforcement, collecting multiple pieces of evidence, including a blanket soaked in blood. This evidence was stored at the Wapello County Sheriff's Office.

The initial investigation focused on discovering Jones' movements immediately before she was killed. Investigators circulated photos of Jones and interviewed many people to try to discover someone who had seen her on that Tuesday.

Jones' landlord, Roy Ware, reported that he'd received a letter from her on Wednesday April 10th, the day after she was killed. It contained her rent check, and told him that she had a new roommate, Lynn Guyette. Guyette was a fellow employee at Henry's Drive-In. When interviewed she said that she'd been living with Jones for around a month.

Police found out about another letter Jones had written on the day she died. Postmarked April 9th, it had been sent to friends back in North Carolina, and told them all about a boyfriend named Art.

Jones told her friends that he didn't want to get married, but had given her a beautiful ring for Valentine's Day. In many cases those closest to the victim are often the first suspects, but in Jones' case police did not believe her boyfriend had been involved.

By the end of the first week after her body had been found, police had identified a suspect. The suspect underwent a polygraph test, but no charges were made. Police indicated that they had strong suspicions as to the guilty party, but that there was not enough evidence for formal charges.

It was discovered that the man who had hassled Jones for a date, Robert Pilcher, was the Marlin's cousin. It was well known in the area that he often brought women to the farmhouse.

Just four days before Jones' murder he had gone there with a waitress that he had picked up from a local bar. Pilcher had allegedly handcuffed her and forced her to perform oral sex on him. Police arrested Pilcher and charged him with sodomy, but no evidence was discovered to link him to Jones' murder.

Pilcher was convicted for sodomizing the barmaid, but the conviction was overturned in 1975 when the Iowa Supreme Court found the law unconstitutional.

Over time the case went cold. Both Jones' family and the Iowa Governor's Office put up money for a reward to try and coax witnesses into coming forward. No one did.

About a year after Jones' murder the evidence was packed up and sent into storage. Years passed and the evidence remained hidden away. Meanwhile, science advanced.

Almost a decade after Jones' murder, a young geneticist in England made the first discovery that would eventually lead science to DNA fingerprinting. Three years later, DNA evidence was used in a courtroom to convict a killer for the first time. By 1998, the FBI started the first national DNA database, CODIS. Jones' case remained cold.

As the years continued passing, one person kept pushing on Jones' case. Her sister, now Judith Cabanillas, kept the pressure on investigators. She kept her own case notes and would pepper them with questions.

In 1995 she traveled to Iowa and arrived unannounced at the Marlin's door, wanting to speak to the woman who found her sister's body. Jones' family also reached out to the media to keep the case in the public eye, particularly around significant anniversaries.

In 2009 the Iowa Division of Criminal Investigation was awarded federal funding to establish a cold case unit. At that time it was estimated that Iowa alone had over four hundred unsolved homicides since 1900, Jones' case being one of them.

Jones' case was chosen by the unit to be investigated. In 2010, the evidence from the crime scene was re-examined, and DNA from the blood-soaked blanket was added to CODIS. It got a hit – Robert Pilcher.

Pilcher had led quite the life after Jones' murder in 1974. He had committed multiple petty crimes, his face being a familiar posting on crime websites. It was these crimes that ensured his DNA was now in the system to be found in 2010.

Police arrested him for Jones' murder at a Des Moines hotel on November 13th, 2012 and charged him with first-degree murder. He was sixty-six years old. Pilcher was transported to the Wapello County Jail, where he was held on bail of $1M, pending his first court appearance. His trial was set for October 13th, 2013. A judge delayed the trial in September 2013 to January 14th, 2014.

At trial, Pilcher's defense was quick to point out that the discovery of his DNA did not mean that he was Jones' killer, as he had taken other women to the farm house for sex prior the night Jones was killed. They noted that other DNA and forensic evidence at the scene, including hair and fingerprints, did not belong to Pilcher.

The defense claimed that Pilcher was working in a Jaycees Circus office when Jones was killed. His lawyer did state that his client's alibi was unable to be confirmed due to how long it had been since Jones' murder. He said that many witnesses were now dead, or could no longer remember accurately that far back.

At the trial, the prosecution introduced a witness who testified that Pilcher had boasted to her about having offed someone years ago in Ottumwa. The witness had been a crack cocaine addict for many years, and even the prosecution admitted that affected her credibility as a witness.

Perhaps then it was not surprising that on January 30th, 2014, Pilcher's trial was ruled a mistrial when the jury could not agree on a verdict. Despite the results, prosecutors were not done with the case. Another trial was scheduled for March 25th, but was then postponed by a request from the prosecutors for a change in venue.

The request was denied and a new trial date set for September 9th, 2014. Midway through, the trial the case was closed abruptly on September 16th when Pilcher pleaded guilty to second-degree murder.

Pilcher was sentenced to ten years in prison at sixty-eight years old. This is similar to the penalty he would have received had he been convicted of murder in 1974. With time served and good behavior, he could be freed as early as 2019.

Current Status:
Detective Wayne Shelton was convinced of Pilcher's guilt and took a personal interest in the case. He continued to work the case on his own long after his retirement. He was still investigating Jones' murder when he died in 2007.

Jones' sister Judith feels that the ten-year sentence is only partial justice. She has been quoted in the media as saying that she wished Iowa had the death penalty.

Along with Jones' case, the cold case unit also solved another high profile case, that of a thirty year old triple murder. The perpetrator was a man who had already been executed for kidnapping and murdering a child in 1987. Despite these successes, when the federal funding ran out in 2011, the Iowa Cold Case Unit was put on ice.

Victim: Nilsa Padilla
Date: April 1985
Location: Key Biscayne, Florida
Suspect: Jorge Walter Nuñez

Backstory:
Nilsa Padilla was born on August 11th, 1958. She grew up in Catano, a poor Puerto Rican fishing town near San Juan. Her parents were both alcoholics, leaving Padilla and her four siblings to mostly fend for themselves. It didn't take long for them to find themselves in trouble.

Padilla's cousin and old friend, Maggie Soto has told the media that Padilla wasn't a good influence. Soto reports that Padilla wasn't what you would call gorgeous, but she had dark hair and eyes that attracted the boy's attention.

She had a bold personality and wouldn't hesitate to introduce herself to boys. Padilla stole candy from the local store and gave it to her friends. Soto described Padilla as wild.

In the summer of 1976, Padilla disappeared overnight, leaving no note or forwarding address. Her brother Radames Mercado said that she had been saving to buy a ticket to New York.

He only heard from his sister one more time in his life. Two years later an envelope was delivered containing just one thing, a photo of his sister holding a baby girl. She looked happy and peaceful.

In reality, Padilla's life was far from serene. She had indeed gone to New York, where she had started dating Miguel Cruz, a much older man who was also Puerto Rican and worked as a mechanic.

Within four months, Padilla was pregnant but the relationship would not last for long. Before her baby could even be born, Cruz was arrested for the rape of two women. When he went to prison, Padilla ended the relationship.

Unfortunately for Padilla, her next relationship was even worse.

On The Day In Question:
On the morning of April 4th, 1985 the sea was rough. A beachcomber walking at dawn noticed the glint of something catching the early morning light. Investigating, he discovered a bulky trash bag that was wedged between two boulders. When he poked a finger through the plastic to see what was inside, he got the shock of his life. Staring back at him was human skin.

Miami-Dade police quickly arrived on the scene and cut open the bag. A body, or parts thereof, spilled gruesomely onto the sand. The head and limbs were missing, the bag containing a young woman's torso.

The discovery would be incredible enough alone, but it was not the first. Just the day before, two fishermen near the Miami Seaquarium tried to rescue what they thought was an injured manatee. Instead of a gentle sea creature when they got close they found a man's rib cage.

Both bodies had marks indicating they had been dismembered with the same instrument. Having no idea of their identity, police nicknamed the bodies "Tommy and Theresa Torso".

Over the next couple of weeks, gruesome finds continued to be reported along the Miami coastline as more body parts washed ashore. The woman's thigh was found in front of a hotel at Sunny Isle Beach, and her leg on Fisher Island. Lastly her head was found still floating in Government Cut, a shipping channel near Miami Beach.

At the time it was the height of the cocaine cowboy era and brutal murders were not uncommon in the city. Even so, the dismembered remains floating ashore set a new grisly standard.

When a hand was found, police attempted to recover fingerprints. They could not understand how no one had reported either person missing. One thing they were almost sure of was that it had to have something to do with the drug trade. It was almost twenty-five years before police discovered how wrong they were.

Investigation:
Years passed, and it was be 2010 before any significant development was made on the case. Charles McCully manned the phone line in the Miami-Dade Cold Case Squad. He usually received around one call a week.

Sometimes it was useful, but more often the call was from someone looking for a long-lost family member or the ramblings of a drunk man boasting about a bogus murder. One guy in particular did this regularly.

So when Gloria Hampton walked into his office that summer, he was suspicious, to say the least. Hampton was twenty-nine years old, short with tanned skin and curly hair.

She told the detective that after years of psychiatric therapy she had uncovered memories of her father killing her mother and placing her in a green bag. Hampton claimed this had happened when she was just four years old.

Her statement didn't help McCully's suspicions any. Recovered memories were already a potential landmine and generally not trusted by law enforcement. Add in that the alleged incident had happened twenty-five years ago, and he was skeptical.

Putting aside his own thoughts, when Hampton left McCully pulled out the cold case files. Hours later he found a thin binder that hadn't been examined for years. Inside were notes from an unsolved murder in 1985, along with a photo of a woman's body in a green trash bag.

DNA tests were organized quickly, and it wasn't long before Theresa Torso was finally identified as Nilsa Padilla, Hampton's mother. From there, her father Jorge Walter Nuñez instantly became the sole suspect.

For the police, a twenty-five year old case was suddenly making headlines again, but for Hampton the discovery meant much more. Ridiculed for years by police, caseworkers and foster parents and called crazy, now she knew she had been right all along.

One piece of the puzzle was unsolved however. Jorge Walter Nuñez was missing, and no one knew where he was.

Police discovered that when he first began a relationship with Padilla, Nuñez had been using the alias Rafael Guzman. Just like her last relationship, he was much older than Padilla at ten years her senior. He also had a history of causing trouble.

Nuñez's father had originally left Peru for the US to become a tailor. When Nuñez was eighteen, his father sent for him. Nuñez arrived in the USA for the first time on July 1st, 1967. His passport showed a nice young man, clean-shaven and smartly dressed. The reality was far more sinister.

Nuñez quickly overstayed his three-month tourist visa. By the time he was twenty-three he had a strong reputation for stealing and lying, and had been arrested in Jamaica for grand larceny. It is not known exactly how he and Padilla met, but he was already a heavy drinker when they did.

Nuñez and Padilla were a couple when he was arrested for grand larceny again in November of 1979, and for stealing in March 1980. However the charges were all dismissed.

In the summer of 1981 Padilla and Nuñez arrived at the house of her cousin, Maggie Soto. The couple had with them their young daughter Bernisa (not Nuñez's biological child), four, and a newborn, Gloria. Soto reports that Nuñez was always drunk, and brought out the worst in Padilla.

Padilla also drank and when she did, she often developed a dark mood. One day Soto witnessed her hit Bernisa over the head with a brush, causing a gash on the child's head. Soto told Padilla she would report her to the police if she hit the children again. Shortly after the incident Padilla and Nuñez left town, heading towards Florida.

Soto next saw Padilla three years later. Having had another child, baby Alicia, the couple was on the run from the Department of Health and Rehabilitation Services in Florida.

Padilla showed Soto an injury to Gloria's hand. She told Soto that Nuñez had dropped a heavy piece of metal onto the toddler's hand. Neither of them had ever taken the child to hospital.

Around the same time, Soto witnessed Nuñez shoving Padilla inside a U-Haul during an argument outside Soto's house. When Soto checked on her, Padilla told Soto that she was tired of Nuñez, and drank to numb depression.

She told Soto that she had no money and so was unable to leave him. Nuñez meanwhile made no effort to hide his hatred for Padilla, telling Soto that one day he was going to kill Padilla.

The family returned to Florida in 1984, parking their U-Haul on Virginia Key Beach. By 1985 they were living there permanently. The island was officially closed, but was used as a popular place to squat and camp by the homeless, drug users and alcoholics.

In April 1985 a horrible secret was be discovered. Whenever Padilla sent Nuñez out to do an errand, he would take Bernisa, the eldest child, with him. During the trip Nuñez would sexually abuse her.

One morning in April, while a drunk Padilla was getting Bernisa ready for school, Bernisa spoke up and told her mother what Nuñez did to her. Instead of comforting and helping her daughter, Padilla smacked Bernisa across the face, leaving her bleeding.

Nuñez had been absent from their camp, and did not return until around 2:00am the next day. Padilla was waiting for him. By the time the sun rose the next day, Padilla was missing. She was never mentioned again. A few weeks later, the youngest child Alicia would also go missing.

The years passed, and the two remaining girls Bernisa and Gloria continued to live in an abusive household. They lived out of the U-Haul parked on a beach. Nuñez didn't work, and any money he did have was spent on beer and drugs.

If Bernisa and Gloria wanted to eat, they had to catch their own food, surviving on shrimp and crab they found in nearby rock pools. Nuñez continued to molest the girls, raping one or both of them daily for years. He also let other men do the same.

The girls were both affected by the years of abuse, but reacted very differently. Bernisa would rarely leave the camp, traveling only to church once a week. In comparison Gloria left nearly every day to escape, disappearing early in the morning and returning at sundown. Every night she would try and convince Bernisa to leave with her, but Bernisa was too afraid.

One day the sisters were looking for food near a local bait shop when Geraldine Mortenson approached them. She asked what happened to the children, and they pointed out the U-Haul where they lived.

Mortenson, who lived in Hollywood with her boyfriend, had traveled from Hollywood to spend some time at the beach. Her heart was touched by the condition the girls were living in, and she returned the following week with clothes and food for them. Her boyfriend drank with Nuñez, distracting him, while she tended to the girls. Eventually she rented an apartment nearby, and the girls visited. One day when Nuñez told them it was time to leave, the girls hid behind Mortenson. Nuñez threatened to kill her if she ever attempted to take his children, and the next time she visited their camp the U-Haul and the family were gone.

Nuñez hid the girls from Mortenson in a local housing project, and Bernisa (who was now eleven years old) began to attend school. One day she invited a friend over, locking her bedroom door to keep her father out.

In the middle of the night the friend woke up to find a Nuñez on top of her. She elbowed him and escaped, reporting the incident to the police.

Nuñez was arrested three days later, telling his children "don't tell them anything" as the police took him away. Police officers tried to get Bernisa to talk, but she denied they had ever been abused. They then talked to Gloria, eight, who told them everything.

Nuñez was convicted of two counts of lewd and lascivious acts on children and was sentenced to four years in jail. By the time he was released the girls had changed their names and vanished.

As if fate itself intervened, in the end Mortenson was the one who took the girls in. They were originally placed in a foster home, but the foster caregiver lost her license and they were placed in a children's shelter.

The shelter staff called Mortenson to see if she was interested in caring for the girls. She immediately drove down and took them home.

Mortenson moved to the Keys so the girls could stay in school, and arranged appointments with psychiatrists for them. Both Bernisa and Gloria drew pictures in crayon of their mother covered in blood.

Psychiatrists dismissed them as images drawn by children suffering from Post-Traumatic Stress Disorder (PTSD). They did not believe the images reflected real life.

Despite this, Mortenson did believe the girls that something terrible had happened to their mother. When Nuñez was going to be released from prison in 1993 she was scared they would be easily found and identified in the small community.

Mortenson let both girls choose a different surname each and then moved them all to Hollywood. To this day she believes that these actions saved their lives.

Bernisa and Gloria had very different personalities even as children, and as they grew these differences impacted their relationship with each other. Bernisa became more religious, but Gloria rebelled.

When she was in Jacksonville for surgery on her damaged hand, Gloria ran away and was missing for two days. She did it again when she was fifteen, this time going missing for over two months. When she was found she was again living with the homeless and this time she was drinking.

When police returned Gloria home, she hardly spoke to her sister. Gloria also felt that they were treated like maids at Mortenson's house. She moved out to an apartment for troubled teens, and by sixteen was pregnant.

Bernisa would marry a nice man named David, but had trouble being intimate. She hadn't let a man touch her since the abuse. He also wanted children and she didn't. With a son to support and no skills or experience, Gloria began stripping in South Miami, drinking to cope.

Throughout the girls' teen years, Nuñez was still living close to the area, usually still squatting with the homeless. Police suspect that he was looking for his children. He was arrested every couple of months for offenses such as being drunk and disorderly or trespassing.

One night, Gloria met a man at the bar where she stripped. His name was Milton Solis, a mechanic who caught her eye and ended up sweeping Gloria off her feet. He helped her quit the club and find another job. The couple even had a son in 2007.

As she put her life back together, Gloria began to investigate what had happened to her mother. She worked at Target and befriended a police officer who worked nights as a security guard. He urged her to talk to homicide investigators.

Gloria tried talking to the police, but investigators dismissed her claims. In the end, she took matters into her own hands. She found prison visitation records for Bernisa's biological father, Miguel Cruz, and tracked him down by calling every possible phone number matching the name. Finally she found him, and he told Gloria they had been looking for Padilla for over twenty-five years.

Gloria got in contact with Maggie Soto, who asked how her sister Alicia was. For Gloria, the question brought up long buried memories of Alicia, and what had happened to her.

A few weeks after Padilla had disappeared, Nuñez was driving to a trailer park to pick up a welfare check. He had given the girls cereal, telling them to eat. Bernisa wasn't hungry and left her bowl full.

When Nuñez returned and asked who hadn't eaten, Bernisa told him that it was Alicia, thinking that he wouldn't hurt the youngest, who was still a baby. Tragically, she was wrong.

Nuñez struck the child over the head so hard that she went limp. She never regained consciousness, and Nuñez disposed of her body. Bernisa and Gloria never saw her again.

After her conversation with Soto, Gloria was determined to find justice. She spoke to the police again, this time mentioning Alicia. Detective McCully subpoenaed state records and, sure enough, there was a record of Alicia Padilla-Gunzman. The child had been born in 1982, and then had simply disappeared, her name never appearing on an official record again. Now police took Gloria's claims seriously and the case of Padilla's disappearance was re-opened.

Bernisa wanted nothing to do with the investigation, but Gloria was keen. In the end, both sisters gave a DNA sample to police, Bernisa saying that she did it for Gloria alone, and not her mother. It was tested and a match was found. The remains of "Theresa Torso" were finally identified as belonging to Padilla.

The elation was short lived. An arrest warrant was issued for Nuñez, only for police to discover he had been deported to Peru in 2004. His Peruvian identification number had expired in 2010 and had not been renewed. Nuñez was either dead, or on the run somewhere in the world.

With the DNA match confirmed, and the long suppressed memories of Bernisa and Gloria pieced together, police believe they now know what happened to Padilla that night.

The night Padilla confronted Nuñez about his abuse of their children they had both been drinking. During the argument, he struck her on the head with a beer bottle, over and over again until the glass broke. Padilla tried to climb out of the camper's back door, but Nuñez shoved her back inside using his foot. He closed the door, and the girls could hear their mother's screams.

Neither sister witnessed Nuñez dismembering their mother's dead body, but Gloria remembers seeing the body parts put into green garbage bags, the army green bags from her memory and the bag the body of Theresa Torso was found in.

Police believe that Nuñez then threw the bags into the ocean from a bridge, believing that the parts would be swept out to sea. Instead, they circled the currents and were eventually washed up into the bay, where they were found.

The next day, he drove the girls to a friend's house, where he gave them mangoes to eat while he washed blood from the U-

Haul. It was just a few weeks later that he killed Alicia, and the years of horror for Bernisa and Gloria began.

Current Status:
Gloria Hampton was furious with police over her father's disappearance. According to records, when she first brought her mother's case to their attention, her father was still in the country and could have been arrested.

Bernisa has not forgiven her mother. She relented to her husband's request to have a child, but the couple divorced just a year later. She is now a single mother.

Gloria and Milton are still together. They have two sons.

South Florida has long been a refuge for drug dealers and drifters. An average of three bodies joins the long list of unidentified dead found in the state every year. Rarely are they ever identified.

Conclusion

It is satisfying to know that the criminals in this book have been caught and have paid or are paying for their crimes. Unfortunately, the families and friends of the victims are still living with the grief and devastation of losing their loved ones. That is a sentence they will have to bear for the rest of their lives.

Hopefully, the fact that the perpetrators have been caught will provide some modicum of solace to them. That and knowing there is no more sorrow, pain or fear for their lost loved ones to bear.

Thank You

Dear Readers,

Thank you for buying and reading my book. I hope you found it interesting and thought provoking.

If you enjoy reading about true crime, please check out my other books, listed at the beginning of the book.

Thank you again and pleasant reading,

Mike Riley

Printed in Great Britain
by Amazon

79333628R20068